WITHDRAWN

A Brief Political and
Geographic History of

Asia

Where Are... Saigon, Kampuchea, and Burma

Mitchell Lane
PUBLISHERS

P.O. Box 196
Hockessin, Delaware 19707
Visit us on the web: www.mitchelllane.com
Comments? email us: mitchelllane@mitchelllane.com

Places In Time
A Kid's Historic Guide to the Changing Names and Places of the World

Titles in the Series

A Brief Political and Geographic History of . . .

Africa
Where Are Belgian Congo, Rhodesia, and Kush?

Asia
Where Are Saigon, Kampuchea, and Burma?

Europe
Where Are Prussia, Gaul, and the Holy Roman Empire?

Latin America
Where Are Gran Columbia, La Plata, and Dutch Guiana?

The Middle East
Where Are Persia, Babylon, and the Ottoman Empire?

North America
Where Are New France, New Netherland, and New Sweden?

Places In Time
A Kid's Historic Guide to the Changing Names and Places of the World

A Brief Political and Geographic History of

Asia

Where Are... Saigon, Kampuchea, and Burma

Doug Dillon

Mitchell Lane
PUBLISHERS

P.O. Box 196
Hockessin, Delaware 19707
Visit us on the web: www.mitchelllane.com
Comments? email us: mitchelllane@mitchelllane.com

Printing   1   2   3   4   5   6   7   8   9

Library of Congress Cataloging-in-Publication Data
Dillon, Douglas, 1943–
    A brief political and geographic history of Asia: where are Saigon, Kampuchea, and Burma? / by Doug Dillon.
        p. cm. — (Places in time: a kid's historic guide to the changing names and places in the world)
    Includes bibliographical references and index.
    ISBN-13: 978-1-58415-623-9 (library bound)
    1. Asia—Politics and government—Juvenile literature. 2. Asia—Historical geography—Juvenile literature. I. Title.
DS33.D55 2007
950—dc22
                                                                        2007000805

PHOTO CREDITS: Maps by Jonathan Scott—pp. 6, 7, 8, 20, 30, 40, 47, 50, 55, 62, 69, 72, 84; pp. 10, 11, 53, 56, 64, 67, 68, 86, 89—Library of Congress; pp. 12, 13, 87, 92, 93, 94—National Archives; p. 14—H. Hung/AP Photo; p. 15—Neal Ulevich/AP Photo; p. 16—JT/AP Photo; pp. 22, 76—JupiterImages; pp. 23, 25, 26, 27, 45—DowntheRoad.org; pp. 32, 34, 37, 49—AP Photo; p. 36—Altsean-Burma/AP Photo; p. 48—Heesung/Creative Commons; p. 52—Mansell/Time Life Pictures/Getty Images; p. 57—Corbis; pp. 59, 60, 65, 66, 70—Barbara Marvis; p. 72—Kaiser Tufail; p. 77—Buddhismus; p. 81—Amar Chandra; p. 82—Owltoucan/Creative Commons; p. 91—U.S. Air Force.

PUBLISHER'S NOTE: This story is based on the author's extensive research, which he believes to be accurate. Documentation of such research is contained on pages 104–106.

The maps created for these books have been thoroughly researched by our authors, who have extensive backgrounds in world history. Every effort has been made to represent close approximations to these places in time.

The internet sites referenced herein were active as of the publication date. Due to the fleeting nature of some web sites, we cannot guarantee they will all be active when you are reading this book.

To reflect current usage, we have chosen to use the secular era designations BCE ("before the common era") and CE ("of the common era") instead of the traditional designations BC ("before Christ") and AD (*anno Domini,* "in the year of the Lord").

PLB

Places In Time

Table of Contents

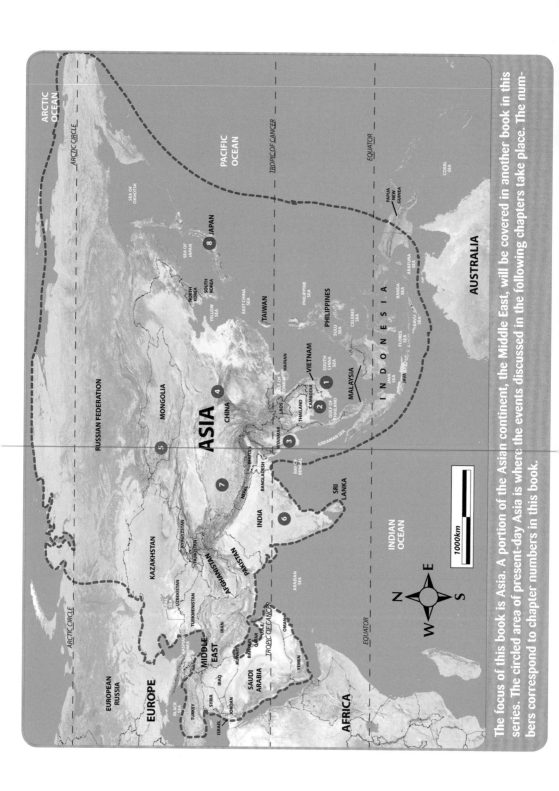

The focus of this book is Asia. A portion of the Asian continent, the Middle East, will be covered in another book in this series. The circled area of present-day Asia is where the events discussed in the following chapters take place. The numbers correspond to chapter numbers in this book.

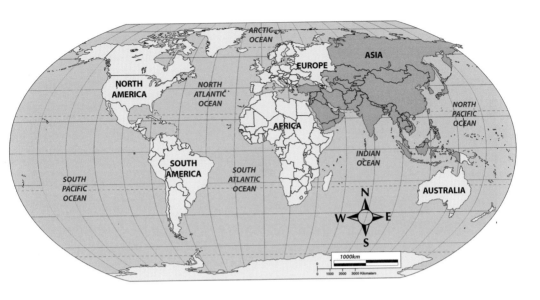

Introduction

The names of places in the world often change over time. This happens to cities, countries, and even larger parts of the earth's surface. Such a shift occurs for many reasons, but usually it is because of war or change in leaders. Whoever is in control of a place gets to name it. Even if most of the people living there do not like that control, the name stays. The flow of history then continues until new leaders have the chance to change the name yet again.

Asia has had many such shifts in its long history. This small book cannot discuss them all, but it does explore some of the most interesting and important. In the eight chapters ahead, you will travel back in time to when these changes happened. These are stories of real people who lived during times that helped make Asia what it is today. The map to the left shows the area on which each chapter concentrates.

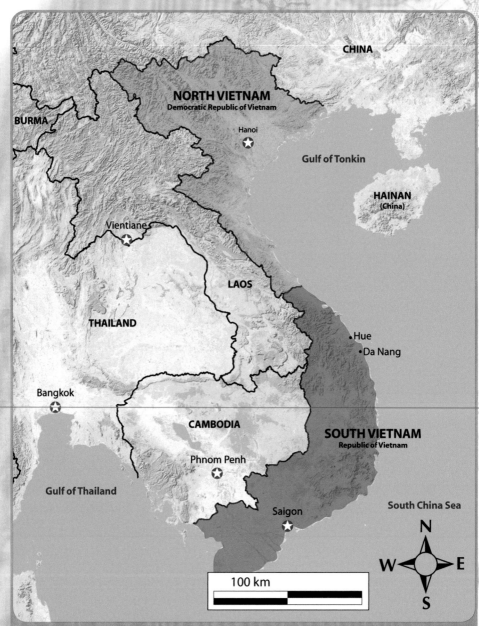

From 1954 to 1976, Vietnam was split into two countries, north and south. During most of those years, there was a terrible war between both nations. In trying to protect South Vietnam from the Communist North and the Viet Cong, the United States lost almost 60,000 soldiers.

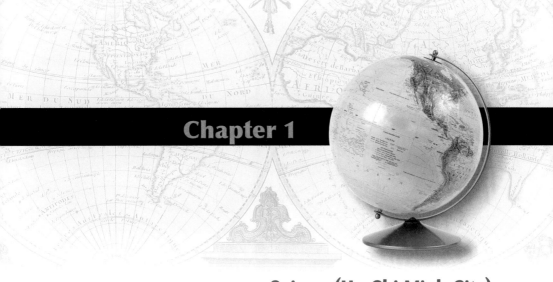

Chapter 1

Saigon (Ho Chi Minh City)

On April 28, 1975, fear and panic raced through Saigon, the capital of South Vietnam. People in the city knew the the huge army from North Vietnam could attack at any minute. Black smoke and explosions in the distance showed just how close the enemy really was.[1] Afraid for their lives, crowds of people fought to leave the city any way they could.

Fighting in that part of the world had been going on for a very long time. Vietnam became French territory in the 1880s, but by 1945, many of its people—led by Ho Chi Minh—demanded their freedom. When France refused to give up control, a war erupted.

In 1954, Ho Chi Minh, a communist, and his forces defeated the French. At that time, an international conference temporarily divided Vietnam into two countries, North and South Vietnam, with Ho as leader of the North. Ho called his country the Democratic Republic of Vietnam.[2]

The idea was for all the people of Vietnam to elect their leaders when it again became one country. That never happened. Many people in South Vietnam didn't like the possibility of being under the communist rule of Ho Chi Minh. Instead of taking part in an election, South Vietnam became the Republic of South Vietnam in 1955.

Ho Chi Minh and the communist north, however, became determined to take over South Vietnam. There were also communists in South Vietnam who wanted their country to join the north. Eventually known as the Viet Cong, these people soon began fighting against the

government of the south. The war for control of South Vietnam had begun.

By 1965, when it looked like the north and the Viet Cong might take over South Vietnam, the United States entered the war as an ally of South Vietnam. The U.S. already had military advisers in the country but it was then that Americans officially started fully fighting against the communists. Fearing the spread of the communist way of life in the world, U.S. President Lyndon Johnson felt he had no other choice.

For eight long years, the United States fought on the side of the South Vietnamese but could never beat the north and the Viet Cong. After nearly 60,000 American soldiers died, the United States decided to quit the war. Early in 1973, President Richard Nixon made peace with North Vietnam. Over the next two months, most American troops left South Vietnam.

Honored by people in Vietnam even after his death in 1969, Ho Chi Minh had been a member of the communist party since 1919. In those early days as a young man and communist agent, he traveled extensively. He even lived for a while in China, France, and the United States.

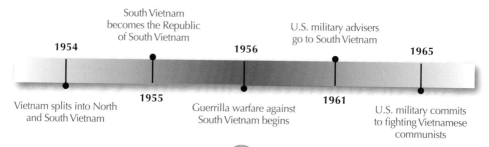

South Vietnam becomes the Republic of South Vietnam

U.S. military advisers go to South Vietnam

1954

1956

1965

Vietnam splits into North and South Vietnam

1955

Guerrilla warfare against South Vietnam begins

1961

U.S. military commits to fighting Vietnamese communists

Because of the American withdrawal, South Vietnam lost most of its territory to North Vietnamese troops and the Viet Cong during the next two years. By March of 1975, nearly all of South Vietnam's army was falling apart. Scared soldiers and their families joined people running away from the communists. As city after city fell to the advancing enemy, highways heading south became jammed with traffic.

On highway 7-B out of the Central Highlands, the communists and mountain tribesmen attacked the fleeing crowds. Some South

The main fighting force of South Vietnam was ARVN, the Army of the Republic of Vietnam. During the Vietnam War, soldiers like these ARVN troops fought the communists alongside United States military units.

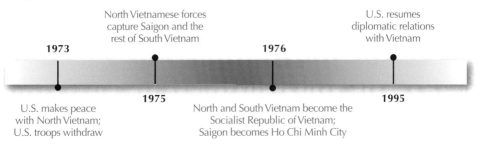

North Vietnamese forces capture Saigon and the rest of South Vietnam

U.S. resumes diplomatic relations with Vietnam

1973

1976

1975

1995

U.S. makes peace with North Vietnam; U.S. troops withdraw

North and South Vietnam become the Socialist Republic of Vietnam; Saigon becomes Ho Chi Minh City

Vietnamese soldiers even fired on their own people. Destroyed vehicles and dead bodies—mostly of women, children, and the elderly—littered the road.[3]

Such scenes of panic were repeated when the communists attacked the cities of Hue and Da Nang. In Da Nang, South Vietnamese soldiers shot their comrades as well as women and children so that they could board the last airplane to leave the airport.[4]

At one time, there were over half a million U.S. troops involved in the Vietnam War. The dense vegetation in Vietnam was hard to move through and was commonly used to set booby traps.

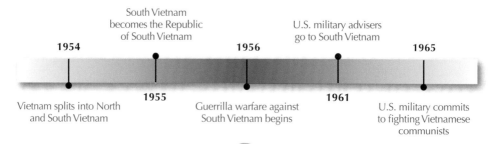

South Vietnam becomes the Republic of South Vietnam

U.S. military advisers go to South Vietnam

1954

1956

1965

1955

1961

Vietnam splits into North and South Vietnam

Guerrilla warfare against South Vietnam begins

U.S. military commits to fighting Vietnamese communists

When Da Nang fell to the communists, the people in Saigon knew it was just a matter of time until North Vietnamese troops attacked their city and took over. Many people did not want to be there when that happened. Some tried to get away by boat.

In an effort to work out a more peaceful change of government, South Vietnamese leaders named General Duong Van Minh as president in late April. At the same time, the United States government rushed to get Americans who remained in Saigon to safety, as well as

In the Vietnam War, the U.S. used bombs containing napalm. Such weapons destroy tree-covered hiding places and kill by burning enemy soldiers to death as well as suffocating them. Innocent civilians died or were badly injured this way as well.

North Vietnamese forces capture Saigon and the rest of South Vietnam

U.S. resumes diplomatic relations with Vietnam

1973

1976

1975

1995

U.S. makes peace with North Vietnam; U.S. troops withdraw

North and South Vietnam become the Socialist Republic of Vietnam; Saigon becomes Ho Chi Minh City

13

the South Vietnamese who worked for them. Anyone who had been very close to the Americans was sure to receive harsh treatment when the North Vietnamese took over.

On April 28, Saigon's airport came under air attack. Explosions shook the buildings where several thousand South Vietnamese waited for evacuation by the Americans. People screamed and ran for cover. The next day rockets and mortars hit the runway, tearing it up. Full of people and under heavy fire, one last airplane barely made it into the air.[5] After the runways closed, U.S. Marines arrived with helicopters to

People rushed to escape as North Vietnam's troops took over cities in the south. Highways became scenes of severe traffic jams. Many refugees died when attacked by communists troops and even scared South Vietnamese soldiers trying to get ahead of everyone else.

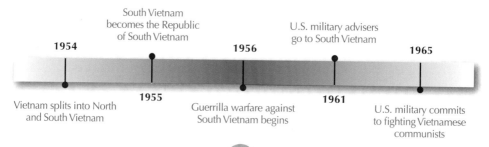

South Vietnam
becomes the Republic
of South Vietnam

U.S. military advisers
go to South Vietnam

1954   **1956**   **1965**

1955   **1961**

Vietnam splits into North
and South Vietnam

Guerrilla warfare against
South Vietnam begins

U.S. military commits
to fighting Vietnamese
communists

People try to climb to safety over the gate at the U.S. Embassy in Saigon, 1975. At the end of the Vietnam War, many Vietnamese people wanted to leave their country. They feared being imprisoned or executed by communist forces.

take the remaining people to ships in the South China Sea. Once the evacuation was complete, communist soldiers moved in and took over the airport.

Things were very tense that evening at the U.S. Embassy in Saigon. In the street outside, a huge crowd of very scared Vietnamese shouted and pushed against the locked gates, hoping to get in. Hundreds more already inside the gates waited to be flown out of the country. The Americans had promised them safe exit from the city.

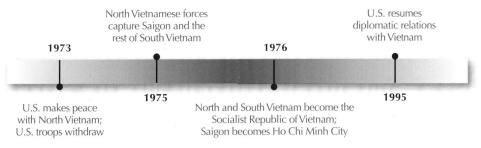

North Vietnamese forces capture Saigon and the rest of South Vietnam

U.S. resumes diplomatic relations with Vietnam

1973

1976

1975

1995

U.S. makes peace with North Vietnam; U.S. troops withdraw

North and South Vietnam become the Socialist Republic of Vietnam; Saigon becomes Ho Chi Minh City

The enemy was close and time was short. Armed U.S. Marines stood guard as helicopters landed and took off in the parking lot and on top of the embassy. The airlift continued into the night with as many Vietnamese as possible taken to the waiting American ships in the South China Sea. However, it was a slow process and everyone became increasingly afraid. Inside the embassy, nervous staff members destroyed documents, leaving nothing of importance for the enemy to find.

Finally, orders arrived from Washington: Only Americans would be able to board the helicopters. The promise to evacuate everyone on the embassy grounds had to be broken. Quickly, Marines shut the embassy doors. Howls of anger erupted from the Vietnamese crowd waiting outside. They banged on the doors and begged to be taken in.

A Marine helicopter crashed on April 29, 1975, on the deck of the USS *Blue Ridge*. Crewmembers carry refugees to safety. At the end of the Vietnam War, the U.S. tried to evacuate Vietnamese people who worked for or helped the Americans.

1954 — Vietnam splits into North and South Vietnam

1955

South Vietnam becomes the Republic of South Vietnam — 1956

Guerrilla warfare against South Vietnam begins

1961

U.S. military advisers go to South Vietnam — 1965

U.S. military commits to fighting Vietnamese communists

Inside, the Americans walked upstairs to the roof and flew to safety. With nearly every American finally gone by 3:00 A.M., including U.S. Ambassador Graham Martin, only a small group of Marines remained.

About five long hours later, one lone helicopter returned for the remaining troops. By then the Vietnamese crowd had broken into the embassy and was trying to get upstairs. As one young Marine thought at the time, "This is where it ends. This is what it feels like to be cornered."[6] He and the other Marines feared they would be killed either by the mob or by communist troops. Only by using tear gas and smoke grenades were the Marines able to keep the crowd back long enough to board the helicopter. With their departure at 7:58 A.M., the United States had officially left Vietnam.

That morning, the city was strangely quiet. There was hardly anyone in the streets. Because they were so afraid, most people stayed indoors. That made it hard for George Asper, a reporter, to find someone to interview. When he finally located a police officer who was willing to talk, the man's eyes were full of fear. He waved his arms around and yelled, "The war is over. We have lost." While Asper took notes, the man kept touching the gun in his holster. This made Asper nervous. Suddenly, the officer turned around, pulled out his gun, and killed himself.[7]

By then it had become clear to everyone that there would not be a big battle for Saigon. The government, the military, and the police had all given up. The enemy was already in the city and there was no point in trying to fight. At the presidential palace, guards had neatly stacked their weapons.[8] President Duong Van Minh quietly waited in his office for the arrival of the communists.

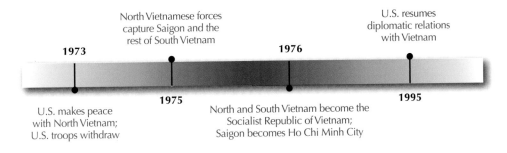

1973 — U.S. makes peace with North Vietnam; U.S. troops withdraw

1975 — North Vietnamese forces capture Saigon and the rest of South Vietnam

1976 — North and South Vietnam become the Socialist Republic of Vietnam; Saigon becomes Ho Chi Minh City

1995 — U.S. resumes diplomatic relations with Vietnam

In the street outside the palace, a North Vietnamese tank rumbled up to the gate and smashed its way through. On top of the tank, a soldier waved a very large communist flag. Other tanks arrived and formed a semicircle with their huge guns pointed at the palace. Quickly, enemy soldiers swarmed into the area. The soldier with the flag jumped down from the tank. Another soldier, also carrying a flag, joined him. The two men raced into the palace and appeared moments later on an upper-floor balcony. When they crisscrossed their flags, the soldiers below fired their weapons in salute and victory.[9] President Minh later went on the radio to announce his surrender. The terrible war that cost over two million Vietnamese their lives[10] had ended. The Republic of South Vietnam was no more.

In 1976, both North and South Vietnam officially reunited to become the Socialist Republic of Vietnam. To honor the leader of North Vietnam, who died in 1969, the city of Saigon became Ho Chi Minh City.

For twenty years after the fall of Saigon to the communists, the United States and Vietnam went their separate ways. Finally, in 1995, U.S. President Bill Clinton officially reestablished the connection between the two countries. In November 2006, U.S. President George W. Bush went to Vietnam and met with its communist leaders. One of the places he visited was Ho Chi Minh City.[11]

Ho Chi Minh City, 2006

Visiting Ho Chi Minh

Even though he died of heart problems in 1969, people still see the famous Vietnamese communist leader Ho Chi Minh in the city of Hanoi. Every week, thousands of visitors walk past his preserved body as it lies in a bulletproof-glass coffin.

Ho's final resting place is at the center of a huge gray mausoleum made of marble. Grim-faced guards stand watch and make sure that people viewing the body follow the rules. Forbidden are cameras or bags of any kind. Also not permitted are talking, photography, and improper clothing like hats, shorts, or sleeveless shirts. People may not put their hands in their pockets.

Ho Chi Minh's Mausoleum in Hanoi

Kept moving by the guards, a single line of people quickly flows past the coffin. Many of the visitors are schoolchildren who come to pay their respects to Vietnam's national hero. Some have tears in their eyes for the lost leader and others giggle, as youngsters everywhere will do. The guards tell them to hush.

Ho Chi Minh was a brilliant and strong leader but a man of simple tastes. "Uncle Ho," as many in Vietnam call him, didn't like to spend money unnecessarily, and he didn't like big, showy ceremonies. He even made it clear in his will that when he died he wanted his ashes to be buried on three hilltops in Vietnam.[12] That, of course, never happened.

Decision makers at the time of Ho's death kept his wishes secret.[13] Instead, they created the very public tomb of today. Now on special holidays, Vietnam's leaders gather there for gigantic parades with marching soldiers and rumbling tanks.

Every October and November, the mausoleum closes down. It is then that Ho Chi Minh's body travels to Russia. Experts there make sure it stays properly preserved for yet another year of tears and giggles.[14]

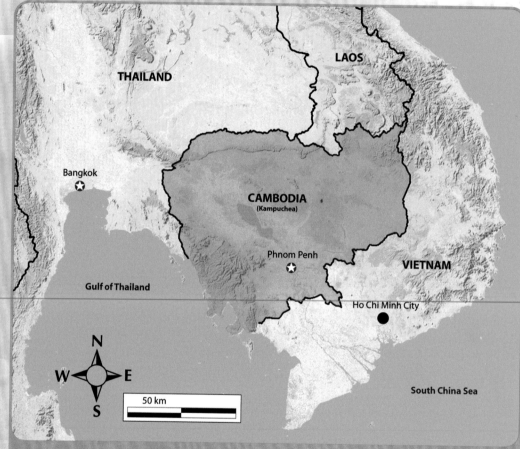

The present-day country of Cambodia once had the name Kampuchea. During those years (1975 to 1989), it was a time of civil war, mass killings, bombings, and finally a takeover by Vietnam.

Chapter 2

Kampuchea (Cambodia)

Not long ago, the present-day country of Cambodia was a place of terror and death. The world looked on in horror as the country of beautiful temples and kind people seemed to have gone crazy. What went on was so terrible it is hard to believe. Cambodia tore itself to pieces.

From 1970 to 1975, half a million people died in a civil war. The next five years were even worse. During that time, at least one out of every seven Cambodians died.[1] For a country about the size of Oklahoma or North Dakota, that period of history is one of bloodiest the world has ever seen.

In 1970, General Lon Nol became Cambodia's leader. He replaced Norodom Sihanouk and Cambodia became the Khmer (kuh-MAIR) Republic. The word *Khmer* came right out of Cambodian history. The ancient Khmer people were ancestors of the present-day Cambodians. They controlled much of Southeast Asia and built many famous temples in the Angkor region of the country. People traveled from all over the world to view these beautiful buildings.

Under Lon Nol's rule, the civil war began. Some people still wanted Sihanouk as leader. Others, called the Red Khmers (or Khmer Rouge), wanted to take over Cambodia. They were Cambodians who wanted to make their country communist ("red") like North Vietnam.

The war in nearby Vietnam caused even more problems. North Vietnam was using eastern Cambodia to supply its fighters in South Vietnam. In addition to that, the Cambodian jungles hid North Vietnamese soldiers who were attacking South Vietnam. Starting in 1969,

The ancient Khmer people built Angkor Wat (above) and other beautiful temples all across Cambodia.

the United States bombed those supply lines and military bases for several years. This, however, just pushed the North Vietnamese deeper into Cambodia.

Meanwhile, the Red Khmers were grabbing big pieces of Cambodia in the civil war. The more they took, the more that people who were opposed to them tried to get away. Phnom Penh (puh-NAWM PEN), the capital, and a few other cities filled up quickly. They were the only places where these people could go.

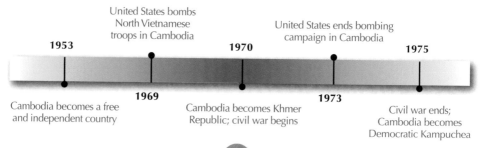

United States bombs North Vietnamese troops in Cambodia		United States ends bombing campaign in Cambodia	
1953		**1970**	**1975**
	1969	**1973**	
Cambodia becomes a free and independent country		Cambodia becomes Khmer Republic; civil war begins	Civil war ends; Cambodia becomes Democratic Kampuchea

The civil war finally ended in April 1975, and the Red Khmer army marched into the capital. The Red Khmer leaders thought that young people could be trusted more than older adults, so most of their soldiers were between the ages of fifteen and twenty. They didn't smile at all.[2] This made some people nervous, but many others were relieved. At least there would be no more war.

Young Red Khmer soldiers stare into the camera. Harsh, unsmiling stares by armed soldiers like these are just part of what the people of Cambodia had to face for four long years.

Very quickly, however, everything changed. All cities in the country must empty for a few days, the Red Khmers said. Go out into the countryside where the food is, people were told. Get out because the Americans might bomb the cities was another reason given. Everyone had to go, even people sick in their hospital beds.

People could not believe what they were hearing, but they had no choice. The unsmiling soldiers might be young, but their weapons were very real. Before long, two to three million Cambodians left the cities. The roads were full of cars, trucks, bicycles, and many people on foot.

It was slow going in the tropical heat. Red Khmers were everywhere guarding the crowds. After miles and miles of travel, the little water and food provided along the way gave out. The travelers started

1979

Vietnamese leave Cambodia
1993

Pol Pot dies
2006

1989

1998

Vietnamese invade Cambodia; name changes to People's Republic of Kampuchea

Cambodia becomes the Kingdom of Cambodia

Surviving Red Khmers are put on trial for war crimes

getting sick and dying. Bodies—mostly of the very old and the very young—soon littered the roadsides.

By the time they arrived in the countryside, it was clear that something was very wrong. The city people realized that they wouldn't be returning home. Then the Red Khmers began executing certain individuals in the crowds—police officers, teachers, anyone who worked for the old Lon Nol government. The situation was starting to look worse than the civil war.

The travelers from the cities realized that the Red Khmers looked at them all as "the enemy." The soldiers even called them a name meaning just that: the New People.

The young communist soldiers were taught that city people were bad and country people were good. The Red Khmers believed that uneducated farmers and village workers were the perfect citizens.[3] Everybody should be like them.

The Red Khmers made the New People build villages and work in the fields to raise rice. Everybody, including children, worked from dawn until well after sunset. It was hard, brutal labor, with pain or death just a heartbeat away. Anybody could be tortured and killed at any moment for almost any reason. As one Red Khmer soldier told some New People, "Keeping you is no profit. Losing you is no loss."[4] The Red Khmers also separated families and sent them in different directions.

To the Red Khmers, religion was bad. For that reason, many religious people were killed. The Red Khmers also didn't like anyone who wore eyeglasses. To them, eyeglasses showed that a person was educated. Educated people were no good, the Red Khmers said, and they

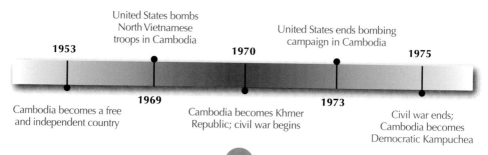

United States bombs
North Vietnamese
troops in Cambodia

United States ends bombing
campaign in Cambodia

1953　　　　　　　　　　　**1970**　　　　　　　　　**1975**

1969　　　　　　　　　　　　　**1973**

Cambodia becomes a free
and independent country

Cambodia becomes Khmer
Republic; civil war begins

Civil war ends;
Cambodia becomes
Democratic Kampuchea

killed them. Very quickly, the New People learned to keep their mouths shut and to get rid of their eyeglasses.

As part of all the changes, the country also received the new name of Democratic Kampuchea (kam-poo-CHEE-uh). In time, it became clear that a man named Pol Pot was the Red Khmer leader. When he took over, Pol Pot said, "Over 2,000 years of Cambodian history has ended."[5] What he meant was that nothing would ever be the same again. He wasn't kidding.

The Red Khmers closed all schools and destroyed all the books in the country. No longer could people own private property, use money, or run a business.[6] Everyone had to have the same kind of clothes and hairstyles.

Within two years, things were going very badly in all of Cambodia. Pol Pot's plans were not working. The New People made terrible farmers and soon there was little rice left anywhere in the country. People were starving, they were dying of disease, and

Pol Pot, the leader of the Red Khmers, became head of Democratic Kampuchea. His rules made life miserable for Cambodians. Close to two million people died during Pol Pot's four years in power. Pol Pot died in 1998, reportedly from heart failure.

there was no medicine.[7] To make things even more confused and difficult, the Red Khmers started killing one another. They had to find

Vietnamese leave Cambodia

1979 **1993** Pol Pot dies **2006**

1989 **1998**

Vietnamese invade Cambodia; name changes to People's Republic of Kampuchea

Cambodia becomes the Kingdom of Cambodia

Surviving Red Khmers are put on trial for war crimes

somebody to blame for the failures. In this way, many Red Khmers died. By 1978, the country was in very deep trouble.

Then the Red Khmers made a fatal mistake. They attacked any Vietnamese people or soldiers still in Cambodia. The Red Khmers even invaded small parts of Vietnam. These actions made the Vietnamese

Under the Red Khmers, treating people horribly became a way of life. Some Cambodians were tortured and drowned in wooden boxes and metal tubs like these.

United States bombs
North Vietnamese
troops in Cambodia

United States ends bombing
campaign in Cambodia

1953 **1970** **1975**

1969 **1973**

Cambodia becomes a free
and independent country

Cambodia becomes Khmer
Republic; civil war begins

Civil war ends;
Cambodia becomes
Democratic Kampuchea

communists very mad. Even though the Red Khmers were also communists, the Vietnamese had to do something to protect their people.

On December 25, 1978, Vietnamese troops invaded Cambodia and easily defeated Pol Pot and his young soldiers. They captured Phnom Penh on January 7, 1979. The Vietnamese renamed the country the People's Republic of Kampuchea. Most of the people in Cambodia welcomed them.[8] The hated Red Khmers were gone.

When Red Khmer soldiers executed people, they often threw their bodies into large pits. These mass graves were discovered many years after the killings stopped.

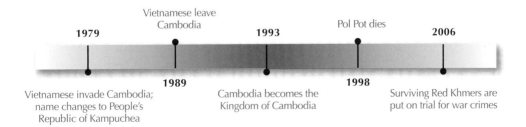

1979
Vietnamese invade Cambodia; name changes to People's Republic of Kampuchea

1989

Vietnamese leave Cambodia

1993
Cambodia becomes the Kingdom of Cambodia

1998

Pol Pot dies

2006
Surviving Red Khmers are put on trial for war crimes

The New People immediately left the farms. Some went right back to the cities, and others walked across Cambodia looking for their relatives and friends. Many even left the country. The rice crop went mostly untouched, which caused even more starvation than before. The Vietnamese had a big job ahead of them in putting the country back together.

For the Cambodians, control by another country, especially Vietnam, got old very quickly. The two countries were ancient enemies, and now the Cambodians wanted the Vietnamese to go home. However, that wouldn't happen for quite a while. After ten years of rule, the Vietnamese finally did leave the country, and it was renamed the State of Cambodia.

In 1993, after help from the United Nations, the country came back to life under a new yet old name: the Kingdom of Cambodia. As such, a king and a prime minister run the country and the people are much happier.

Now that peace has returned to Cambodia, the country is once again a popular travel destination. Foreign tourists visit the cities and ancient temples that not too long ago were mostly deserted. Horrible reminders of the past are also on view for these visitors and local people alike: the stacked bones and skulls of those who died when Pol Pot was the ruler. For many people in Cambodia, memories of the two million people killed by the Red Khmers are still very much alive.[9]

A Child's Journey into Terror

Loung Ung was only five years old when the Red Khmers took over Cambodia. What happened after that would fill her mind with horror and change her life forever.

Loung was playing in the streets of Phnom Penh as Red Khmer soldiers entered the city. The people watching, she recalls, were smiling and cheering at first. They were happy that the long civil war had ended. Very soon after that, everything changed.

When Loung got home, she found her family packing to leave. Everyone was rushing around and she didn't understand why. Soon

Loung Ung survived the terrors of the Red Khmers.

they were all on a crowded road in her father's truck. Everywhere, Red Khmer soldiers shouted at them to leave the city and fired guns into the air.

For the next five years, Loung would struggle to survive. She would see things that no child should ever have to witness. Forced by the Red Khmers to work long days with little food, Loung and her family neared starvation. At times, they ate bugs, frogs, and grasshoppers because there was nothing else. She even watched other people fight over a dead animal in the road so they could cook and eat it.

Time after time, the Red Khmers killed people around Loung whom they thought might be enemies. The jungle often smelled of dead bodies.

When the Red Khmers took her father away, Loung cried and screamed. She knew they would execute him like all the others. By the time the Vietnamese finally defeated the Red Khmers, Loung had lost not only her father but her mother and two sisters as well.

Today, Loung is an adult who lives and works in the United States. She wrote a book called *First They Killed My Father* to tell the world about those long, horrible years when the Red Khmers ruled Cambodia.

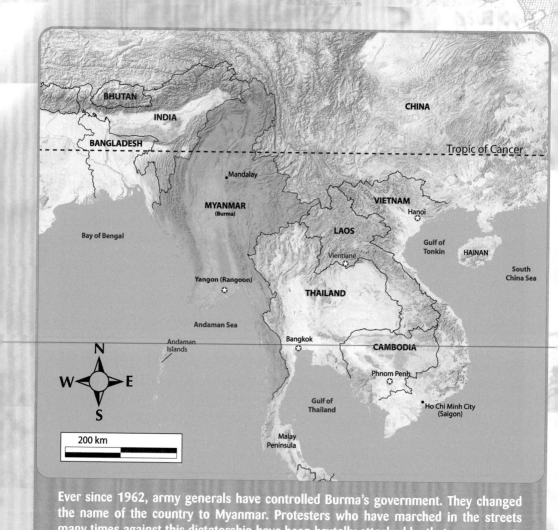

Ever since 1962, army generals have controlled Burma's government. They changed the name of the country to Myanmar. Protesters who have marched in the streets many times against this dictatorship have been brutally attacked by that government.

Chapter 3

Burma (Myanmar)

The country of Burma used to be one of the richest in Southeast Asia. All that changed in 1962 after a new government took over. In time, Burma became one of the poorest countries in the region. There was no election back in 1962 to make that change in government. Instead, the military stepped in and grabbed power. In a short time, a group of generals led by Ne Win turned the country into a dictatorship.

Newspapers could no longer print what they wanted. It was also against the law for political parties to exist. The people had to obey the government no matter what it did. Most of the Burmese people were not happy with those changes, but they could do little about them. To disagree with the new leaders would put their freedom or even their lives in danger.

In an effort to help, many nations protested what the new leaders were doing. To make their point clear, those nations stopped trading with Burma[1] but the generals wouldn't listen. They just closed Burma off from the rest of the world until its wealth became a shadow of what it once was.

Living under military control was like going back in time for the people of Burma. They had a long history of not being able to elect their leaders, and they didn't like this. Starting in 1886, the country was under British rule for many years. The Japanese controlled Burma for a while during World War II. The British returned when the war ended in 1945, but they soon decided to give Burma its independence.

Burma became a free country in January 1948. A written constitution made electing the country's leaders the law of the land. For almost fifteen years after that, people enjoyed the freedoms of democracy. Then the generals took over.

In 1974, Ne Win and his friends retired from the military, but they stayed in control of Burma. Again, there were no elections. The old generals just wrote another constitution that allowed them to stay in power. They even changed the country's name to the Socialist Republic of Burma. These events didn't sit very well with most people in the country, but they had no way to make things better.

Ne Win (right) was the leader of the army generals who took over Burma without an election in 1962. Harsh rule by Ne Win and his friends brought gigantic protests by people across Burma in 1988.

As the years passed, the citizens of Burma disliked what was going on in their country even more. People saw their government as increasingly dishonest and controlling. Burmese citizens felt that they had to be very careful about whom they talked to and what they said. They believed that spies for Ne Win were everywhere.[2]

There were many hated rules. One such rule made people use government Form #10. This new regulation was actually a way to control travel. It said that if you were going to leave home overnight, you had to report it to the government on Form #10.[3]

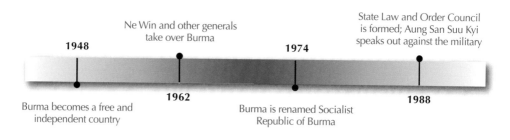

| 1948 | Ne Win and other generals take over Burma | 1974 | State Law and Order Council is formed; Aung San Suu Kyi speaks out against the military |

Burma becomes a free and independent country

1962

Burma is renamed Socialist Republic of Burma

1988

Other rules changed the type of money used in the country. As a result, many people lost all their savings.

By March 1988, many people in Burma had had enough. Anger at their government began to boil over. Twenty-six years of harsh rule by Ne Win and the generals brought people out into the streets to protest. They wanted things to change. It started with students, but then many other types of people such as Buddhist monks joined them. The protests began in Rangoon, the capital. Soon they spread city by city to other parts of Burma.

The government answered the protesters with force. Armed soldiers beat people and arrested them. Over two hundred people lost their lives, including forty-one students who died in a van from lack of oxygen.[4]

This harsh response made people in Burma even angrier. To calm things down, Ne Win resigned as leader of the country but still left the military in control. The government said it forced him to resign, but not many people accepted that story. Some even suspected that Ne Win was still giving orders. Even so, this change gave people a little hope. They thought they just might be winning.

On August 8, 1988, hundreds of thousands of people marched in the streets of Rangoon and other cities. The protesters called for an end to military rule and demanded elections. Soldiers killed, beat, and arrested many thousands of people. In streets all over Burma, the bodies of protesters lay in pools of blood. In turn, some protesters killed people they thought were spies for the military rulers.

Carefully watching all of this was a woman with a very well known name. Aung San Suu Kyi (Oung san soo chee) had come back to her country several months earlier to care for her seriously ill mother. She

NLD party wins election
but does not take power

1989

2006

1990

Country is renamed Myanmar;
Aung San Suu Kyi is arrested

Aung San Suu Kyi remains
under house arrest

Burmese soldiers attack the crowds asking for democracy. Protests against the military in Burma often became violent. Many people were injured, put in jail, and even killed.

had been living in England with her husband and two children for many years.

Aung San Suu Kyi was the daughter of Aung San, a very famous and important man to the Burmese. To many people, Aung San seemed like a father—the father of their country—similar to George Washington in the United States. Like George Washington, Aung San created his country's army. His efforts in the 1940s played an important role in forcing the British out of Burma and giving the country its first constitution. Aung San's enemies assassinated him in 1947, about six

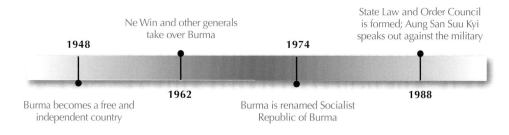

Ne Win and other generals
take over Burma

State Law and Order Council
is formed; Aung San Suu Kyi
speaks out against the military

1948

1974

Burma becomes a free and
independent country

1962

Burma is renamed Socialist
Republic of Burma

1988

months before his country become independent.

When people found out that Aung San's daughter was back in the country, they were delighted. This was their chance, they thought, to spark a return to elections and rid the country of its military leaders. Pro-democracy groups invited Suu Kyi to speak at a huge rally on August 26, less than three weeks after the protests had begun. She accepted and spoke to over one half million people. That talk won the hearts of freedom-loving people in Burma. Her words about human rights and a return to elections were just what they wanted to hear. However, she also told the huge crowd not to try forcing a change in the government by using violence.[5]

Called by many the George Washington of Burma, General Aung San was the main force in making his country independent. He built Burma's army and helped form a constitution. Aung San and most of his cabinet were assassinated in 1947.

The government ignored Suu Kyi's words about democracy. Instead, it took even tighter control of the country. On September 18, 1988, a special military group called the State Law and Order Restoration Council (SLORC) was set up to run the country. This made people furious and they again took to the streets. Once more, soldiers killed

NLD party wins election
but does not take power

1989   2006

1990

Country is renamed Myanmar;   Aung San Suu Kyi remains
Aung San Suu Kyi is arrested   under house arrest

Aung San Suu Kyi speaks to over a million people on August 26, 1988, in the capital city, Yangon. Just a few weeks later, the military would establish the State Law and Order Restoration Council (SLORC), which banned political gatherings of more than four people. Defying the ban, Suu Kyi continued to make speeches to large audiences throughout the country.

many of the protesters. In fear for their lives, people in great numbers fled into the jungles or to other countries.

To keep things from getting out of control again, the SLORC announced some changes. It became legal to form political parties. The SLORC even agreed to hold elections for May of 1990. This was all good news, but there was one problem. It became illegal for people

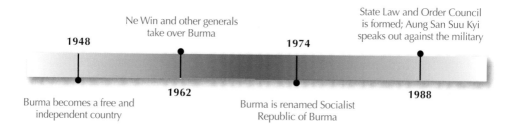

Ne Win and other generals
take over Burma

State Law and Order Council
is formed; Aung San Suu Kyi
speaks out against the military

1948

1974

1962

1988

Burma becomes a free and
independent country

Burma is renamed Socialist
Republic of Burma

to gather in large groups. This made it very hard for political parties to operate. It seemed as if the generals thought they could control the election and win the vote.

Suu Kyi and her friends quickly set up their own political organization. They called it the National League for Democracy (NLD). Even though people were not supposed to gather in groups, Suu Kyi started making speeches all over Burma. Soldiers followed her everywhere but took no action. At first, the SLORC didn't want to seem too tough on the daughter of the great hero, Aung San.

Aung San Suu Kyi (center) stands with supporters of her National League for Democracy party in 1996. Suu Kyi's efforts to return her country to democracy have often put her in great danger. Since 1989, she has been under house arrest more years than not.

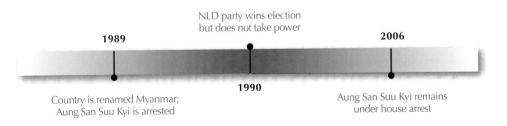

NLD party wins election but does not take power

1989

2006

1990

Country is renamed Myanmar; Aung San Suu Kyi is arrested

Aung San Suu Kyi remains under house arrest

After her mother died in late 1988, the SLORC put great pressure on Suu Kyi. The more popular she became, the more they worked to stop her from criticizing the government. A group of soldiers even came very close to shooting her the following year.[6]

Also in 1989, the SLORC changed Burma's name to Myanmar and the name of its capital to Yangon. In July, the SLORC made a move against Suu Kyi and sent soldiers to her home. They immediately cut all the phone lines and put her under house arrest.

The only way Suu Kyi could leave her home was to leave Burma for good. This she refused to do, and she remained under house arrest on and off for ten of the next seventeen years.

When Suu Kyi's NLD party won the election of 1990, the SLORC didn't like the results. Instead of turning power over to the NLD party, the generals stayed in control. As of 2007, a group of generals was still running Myanmar, as they call it. The United States and many other nations have never recognized the name Myanmar. Most people continue to call the country Burma.

In 1991, Suu Kyi received the Nobel Peace Prize for her efforts to make peaceful changes in her country. In May of 2006, the generals extended Suu Kyi's confinement to her home for yet another year.[7]

The Lady and the Soldiers

When speaking of Aung San Suu Kyi, most people in Burma simply call her "The Lady."[8] The name reflects the great love and respect the people have for her. They have felt this way for many years.

Suu Kyi's calm bravery in pushing for democracy in Burma has won her much admiration at home and across the world. However, her courage to speak out against military control of her country has put her health and safety in danger many times.

Ever since 1988, the military leaders of Burma have kept a close eye on The Lady. They have pressured her to stop talking about democracy or to leave the country. She has always refused to do either one. These refusals have made the generals very angry. For Suu Kyi, this has meant years of house arrest and soldiers constantly nearby.

Once, Suu Kyi faced almost certain death from Burma's military. It was just before the country's elections in April 1989. Suu Kyi was traveling and speaking to people across Burma about democracy. While walking down a road in the village of Danubyu, she and her supporters stopped suddenly. Soldiers in a jeep had driven up and were blocking the way.

This was no ordinary roadblock. The soldiers were crouched with their loaded guns pointed directly at Suu Kyi and those around her. Their leader, a captain, threatened to open fire. Suu Kyi waved all of her supporters away. Then, very calmly and all alone, she walked toward a possible hail of bullets.[9] At the very last second, a major, who outranked the captain, ran up and ordered the soldiers to put their weapons down.

Aung San Suu Kyi had shown her supporters how to live by the words she once shared with the world: "You should never let your fears prevent you from doing what is right."[10]

Aung San Suu Kyi stands in front of her father's portrait.

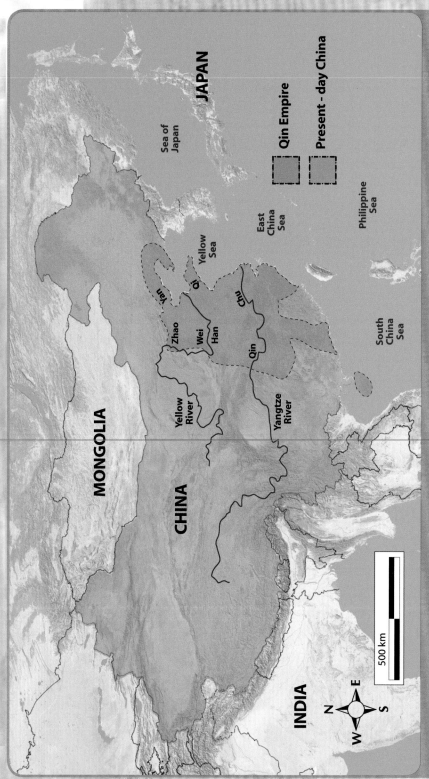

MONGOLIA

CHINA

Yellow
River

Yangtze
River

Zhao
Yan
Wei
Han
Qi
Qin
Chu

Yellow
Sea

Sea of
Japan

JAPAN

East
China
Sea

South
China
Sea

Philippine
Sea

INDIA

N
W · E
S

500 km

Qin Empire

Present - day China

What is now the country of China began with the Qin Empire in 221 BCE. The first Qin emperor united the region into one nation by force. The main rivers through the region are the Yellow (or Huang) and the Yangtze (or Chang). The course of the Yellow River has changed many times throughout the centuries.

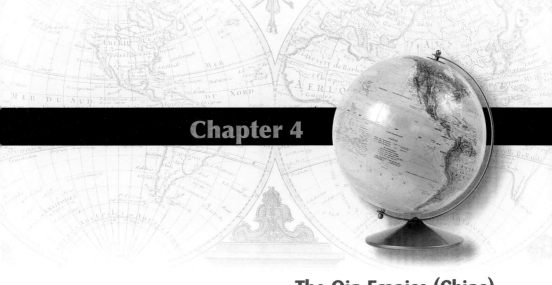

The Qin Empire (China)

More than 2,200 years ago, a thirteen-year-old boy named Ying Zheng became king of a small region in Asia called Qin (pronounced CHIN). Some people spell it Ch'in. At first, the young king didn't know how to rule. A few top leaders in his government made the decisions. In time, however, Zheng learned how to be a strong leader. He would prove his ability years later when he created the beginnings of the country the world now knows as China.

Zheng's kingdom of Qin wasn't very big. It was just one of many such small territories in that area of Asia. For years, these territories were always fighting and trying to conquer each other. Historians call this time in Chinese history the Warring States Period. By 230 BCE, there were only six kingdoms left besides Qin: Zhao, Han, Wei, Chu, Yan, and Qi.[1]

Zheng, who was at that time about thirty years old, decided to put an end to all those little wars. His plan was to force the other six kingdoms to be under Qin control and give them one overall form of government. If they were together under his leadership, Zheng believed, they could also more easily defend themselves from invaders. To accomplish his goals, Zheng sent Qin's strong army against the other kingdoms. By 221 BCE, he had conquered them all and created the Qin Empire. In time, his armies even invaded as far as present-day Vietnam.[2]

As Qin leader, Zheng declared himself "The First Emperor" of all the old territories. His full title in Chinese became Qin Shi Huangdi.

Qin Shi Huangdi, China's first emperor, commanded that his country have one common language, one standard type of money, and that people measure things the same way. He also burned most of the books.

The new emperor didn't waste any time putting his plans into action. He made the Qin city of Xianyang (shan-YAHNG) his capital and started forcing people to do what he wanted.

One of the first things Shi Huangdi did was to break the power of all the royal leaders in the old kingdoms. He did this by moving those people and their families by the thousands to his capital city in Qin. He concluded that he could keep an eye on them there and they couldn't cause trouble back in their old territories. Shi Huangdi didn't want any competition.

Next, the emperor split his empire into thirty-six districts. This wiped out the idea of the old kingdoms for good. Each district had counties and its own governor appointed by the emperor. Families also had to organize into groups of five to ten. These groups were responsible to the emperor for the conduct of each member.

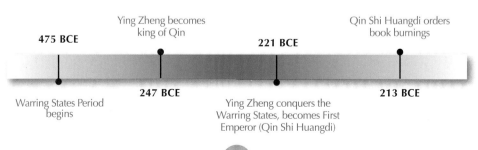

475 BCE

Ying Zheng becomes king of Qin

221 BCE

Qin Shi Huangdi orders book burnings

Warring States Period begins

247 BCE

Ying Zheng conquers the Warring States, becomes First Emperor (Qin Shi Huangdi)

213 BCE

Up until this point, money, language, and measurement in all the old kingdoms had been very different. To pull his empire together, Shi Huangdi did several things. One was to create a single type of money for use by the people in all of his districts. This was a circular coin with a square hole in the center.[3] Next, he commanded the use of the Qin way of speaking and writing across his empire.[4] This became China's first national language, at least for well-educated people and government officials. Shi Huangdi also created one standard way of weighing and measuring things.

Rich or poor, everyone had to obey the emperor or face the

In the Qin Empire, people could use only one kind of money: bronze coins with a square hole in the middle. The square represented the earth and the circular coin represented heaven. These coins were often strung together to make larger units of money.

consequences. To enforce his orders, Shi Huangdi used the police and the military. Anyone who spoke out against how things were done or who broke the law was in deep trouble. Many such people ended up doing hard labor at one of the emperor's building projects. Others had a body part cut off or lost their lives to the executioner. Shi Huangdi once had 460 of his citizens buried alive.[5] These were some of the most educated and important people in the empire.

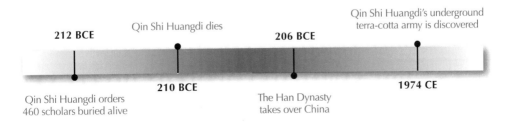

212 BCE

Qin Shi Huangdi dies

206 BCE

Qin Shi Huangdi's underground terra-cotta army is discovered

210 BCE

1974 CE

Qin Shi Huangdi orders 460 scholars buried alive

The Han Dynasty takes over China

Burying those scholars alive also showed Shi Huangdi's dislike for education. The only schooling the emperor wanted in his lands was training government officials to do their jobs. He also ordered the burning of most of the books in the empire.

During this time, it became illegal for anyone to own weapons. Using the tools of war he took from people, the emperor created twelve immense bronze statues. He placed these statues outside the huge new palace he ordered built as a sign that there would be no more war among the old kingdoms.

His new palace was only one of the emperor's many building projects. Canals, new roads, and forts appeared everywhere. To keep invaders out of the Qin Empire, Shi Huangdi ordered the construction of the first Great Wall. The material for the building of this barrier was very simple: tightly compacted dirt. More than 1,500 years later, during China's Ming period, this wall would be replaced by the one built of brick and stone we know today. All of this building took the forced labor of hundreds of thousands of people. Many of them died while working for the emperor.

This new way of life for all the people in the Qin Empire became like a wheel with Shi Huangdi in the middle.[6] The spokes of the wheel were his control going out into every district and home in the empire.

Once when the emperor wasn't able to cross a river, he got very angry. When he demanded to know why he couldn't cross, he got a strange answer. An adviser told him that a goddess living on a nearby mountain had created the problem. This made Shi Huangdi even angrier. He sent 3,000 prisoners to that mountain and had them cut down every tree.[7] No one, not even a goddess, was supposed to get in the emperor's way.

475 BCE	Ying Zheng becomes king of Qin	221 BCE	Qin Shi Huangdi orders book burnings
	247 BCE		213 BCE
Warring States Period begins		Ying Zheng conquers the Warring States, becomes First Emperor (Qin Shi Huangdi)	

Death and spiritual things were of great interest to Shi Huangdi. If there was a way to escape dying, he wanted to find it. For years, he sent people out looking for Peng La, a land where everyone was supposed to live forever. He never found it, of course. However, he did build a huge burial place for himself with thousands of life-sized clay soldiers to protect him after he died.[8]

Death finally caught up with Shi Huangdi in 210 BCE. This happened, strangely enough, soon after the emperor returned from a trip

When the first emperor of China died, workers buried 8,000 soldiers made of hardened clay in front of his tomb. The idea was for these soldiers to protect the emperor forever, using the actual weapons buried with them. Before this time when an emperor died, it was often the custom to sacrifice real people instead of using clay figures.

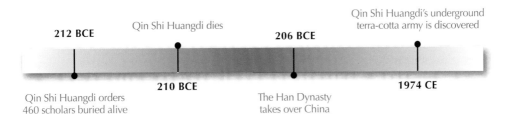

212 BCE

Qin Shi Huangdi dies

206 BCE

Qin Shi Huangdi's underground terra-cotta army is discovered

210 BCE

1974 CE

Qin Shi Huangdi orders 460 scholars buried alive

The Han Dynasty takes over China

to the China coast, where he hoped to find a magic potion of everlasting life. When he died, his empire had only been in existence for about twelve years.

The Qin Dynasty, or rule by the Qin royal family, continued only for a short time. As Qin Shi Huangdi had planned, his oldest son succeeded him and became the Second Emperor. However, a struggle for power began within the royal family. The Second Emperor was soon murdered. In a few short years, all of Shi Huangdi's close family and advisers were dead.

Many citizens of the empire had suffered greatly under Shi Huangdi's rule. The waste in lives destroyed and money spent was just too much. Revolts broke out across the empire. The Qin army and its leaders came under attack. After the final defeat of the Qin army by Prince Liu Bang of the Han people, China's first empire came to a complete end.

A new empire arose from the ashes of the old one in 206 BCE. After taking control of the Qin territories, Liu Bang founded the Han Dynasty. Learning from Shi Huangi however, the Han used many of his laws and regulations. Like the First Emperor, the Han also wanted a unified country. They were much more successful than Shi Huangdi had been. The Han dynasty lasted over 400 years.

Liu Bang was a poor peasant before he became Emperor Gaozu, the first emperor of the Han Dynasty.

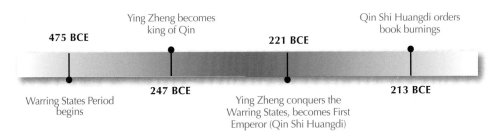

475 BCE

Ying Zheng becomes king of Qin

221 BCE

Qin Shi Huangdi orders book burnings

Warring States Period begins

247 BCE

Ying Zheng conquers the Warring States, becomes First Emperor (Qin Shi Huangdi)

213 BCE

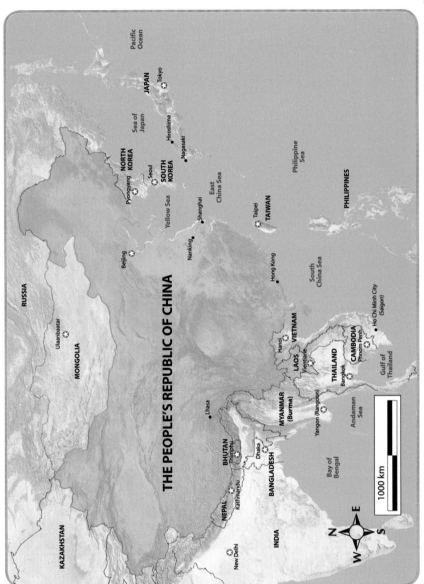

From the Qin Empire over 2000 years ago, the present-day country known as the People's Republic of China (PRC) eventually developed. Shown here is the PRC and surrounding nations as they are today.

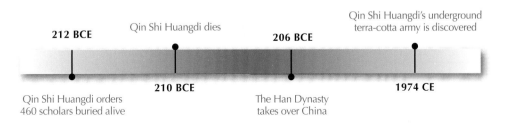

212 BCE

Qin Shi Huangdi dies

206 BCE

Qin Shi Huangdi's underground terra-cotta army is discovered

Qin Shi Huangdi orders 460 scholars buried alive

210 BCE

The Han Dynasty takes over China

1974 CE

Tombs from the Han Dynasty. The Han Dynasty ruled China from 206 BCE to 220 CE.

Many rulers have controlled China over the years since the Han Dynasty. They have come and gone, but one thing is certain: Their power has been firmly rooted in Shi Huangdi's accomplishments in founding the Qin Empire.

China in the twenty-first century is one of the strongest and most important nations in the world. Governed by the communists, its official name is the People's Republic of China (PRC). With well over one billion citizens, the PRC is the most populous country on earth. If he could visit his country today, Qin Shi Huangdi would no doubt smile and nod his approval.

The Emperor's Clay Warriors

Qin Shi Huangdi wanted to continue to rule even after he died. To do this, he set up his burial place much like a very small city on four acres of land.[9] From his tomb within that city, he hoped he could at least rule a tiny kingdom after his death. Construction of the emperor's final resting place required the labor of 700,000 men as well as much of his kingdom's wealth.

People in China have known about Shi Huangdi's tomb and little city for many centuries. Lost to memory, however, was the fact that an entire army lay underground to guard the emperor's body. This army was made of hardened clay called terra-cotta.

In 1974, workers were drilling wells near the tomb when they found big pieces of what looked like pottery and bronze weapons.[10] Since then, three huge pits full of life-sized clay soldiers, chariots, horses, and even real weapons have been uncovered. In all, more than 8,000 clay soldiers have once more seen the light of day.

Today, they still stand guard in earthen ditches dug over 2,000 years ago. Some of the figures are standing, others are crouching or kneeling, and still others are riding horses or driving chariots. Since no two figures are exactly alike, experts think that artists used actual soldiers as models when they created them. Different clothing, hairstyles and facial expressions help make the figures seem almost real.

Pottery brick floors lie beneath the feet of the clay soldiers. Above their heads a steel structure like a huge airplane hangar has been constructed to protect them from the weather.[11] The site is one of China's most popular tourist attractions. More than one million visitors see the terra-cotta warriors every year.

Terra-cotta warriors and horses ready for war

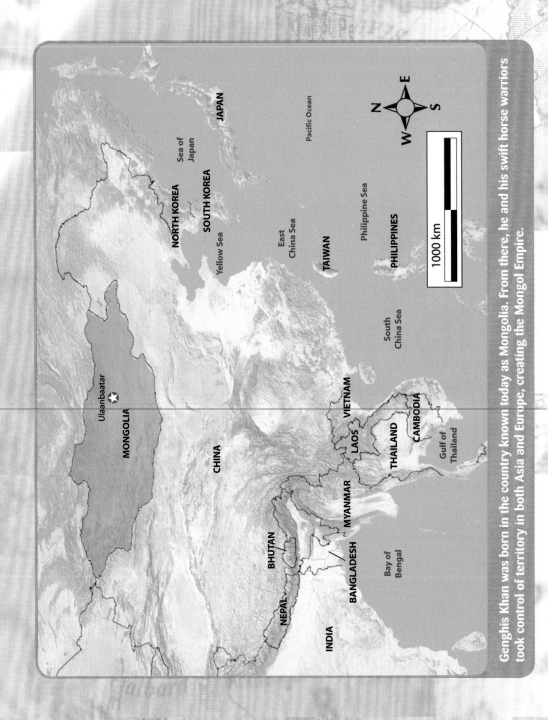

Genghis Khan was born in the country known today as Mongolia. From there, he and his swift horse warriors took control of territory in both Asia and Europe, creating the Mongol Empire.

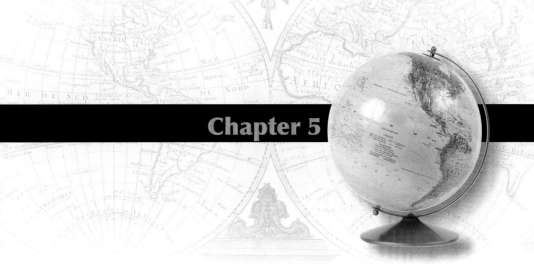

Chapter 5

The Empire of the Great Khan

During the thirteenth century A.D., a wave of change swept through most of Asia. Empires rose and fell and millions of people lost their lives. The change was so powerful that it even swamped parts of Europe a continent away.

It all began in and around the present-day country of Mongolia. The tribal people of that region were fierce, nomadic, and lived in tents. The men were horse warriors who had little respect for the farms and cities of their Chinese neighbors to the south. However, they liked to raid those places in order to take whatever they needed. This they did despite the earthen Great Wall built by Chinese Emperor Qin Shi Huangdi.

When the Mongols and other nearby tribes weren't attacking farms and cities to the south, they often fought each other. This way of life worked for many generations, but toward the end of the twelfth century, one man changed it all. The great Mongol leader Temüjin (TEH-myuh-jun) conquered the other tribes or made alliances with them. In the place of the old way of life, he created a kingdom of the nomadic people.

In the year 1206, all of the Mongol tribal chiefs gathered and named Temüjin as their leader. The name given to tribal rulers in that region of the world was Khan (KAHN). Temüjin then became the Great Khan of all the tribes, with the name Genghis Khan (GENG-guss KAHN). Translated, *Genghis Khan* means "Universal Ruler."[1]

In his push to create the Mongol Empire, Genghis Khan often gave cities he wanted to conquer a choice. They could either join him as an ally or face death and destruction. Eventually, the Mongol Empire stretched from the Pacific Ocean to the Caspian Sea.

Laws under the Great Khan were simple, and they applied to everybody. Punishment for breaking these laws was severe. Usually it was death.

Genghis Khan was a true military genius. He soon organized the Mongols into one of the most powerful and successful armies in history. The fierce horsemen were loyal to the Great Khan and very well disciplined. They formed a tough, swift cavalry that could travel for days existing only on horse milk.[2]

In 1211, Genghis Khan pointed his army south into the Chin Empire of northern China. In their first battle, a much smaller Mongol force destroyed an army of 70,000 in a matter of hours. A monk traveling in that area nine years later reported human bones still scattered everywhere. Within two years, Genghis had conquered 90 cities.

When the people of the Chin capital refused to give up in 1215, he burned the city and killed all of its residents. The streets were full of bodies and slick with human fat from the intense heat.[3] The message to all other cities in the future was that to resist was to die. As brutal as

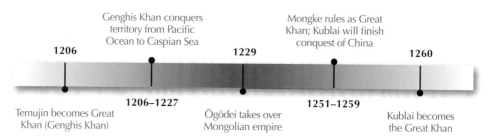

| 1206 | Genghis Khan conquers territory from Pacific Ocean to Caspian Sea | 1229 | Mongke rules as Great Khan; Kublai will finish conquest of China | 1260 |

1206–1227
Temujin becomes Great Khan (Genghis Khan)

Ögödei takes over Mongolian empire

1251–1259

Kublai becomes the Great Khan

Genghis Khan was, he did make allies of the people in cities that surrendered to him peacefully.

Instead of conquering all of the Chin Empire, however, Genghis Khan stopped short. No longer continuing south, he sent his armies toward the west. Soon Genghis was in control of all Central Asia, and he even invaded Russia.

By his death in 1227, the Mongol Empire stretched over two continents, Asia and Europe, from the Pacific Ocean to the Caspian Sea. Never before had so much territory been under the control of one man. With the passing of Genghis Khan, his four sons took over and divided the empire among them. What territory was yet to be conquered in China also became part of this division. The Great Khan made his sons promise to finish that conquest and add it to the empire.

The idea was to give each son a share of the present and future empire but keep it connected under one leader. That new leader was Genghis's son, Ögödei. As the next Great Khan, Ögödei inherited the most important piece of the Mongol Empire. His share

Ögödei, the third son of Genghis Khan, promised to conquer the rest of China for the Mongol Empire. As he worked to fulfill this promise, he also finished building Karakorum, capital of the Mongolian Empire until the 1270s.

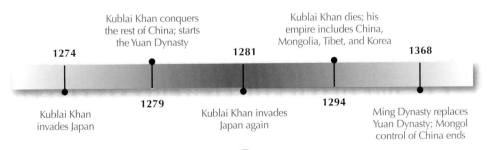

Kublai Khan conquers the rest of China; starts the Yuan Dynasty

Kublai Khan dies; his empire includes China, Mongolia, Tibet, and Korea

1274

1281

1368

1279

1294

Kublai Khan invades Japan

Kublai Khan invades Japan again

Ming Dynasty replaces Yuan Dynasty; Mongol control of China ends

of those lands included Mongolia, as well as conquered and yet-to-be-conquered Chinese lands. The name of that vast territory was the Empire of the Great Khan.

In the following years, Ögödei Khan continued to combine forces with his brothers in conquest. Together they expanded the Mongol Empire much as their father had hoped. In 1234, they conquered what was left of the Chin Empire. They also pushed deeper into Russia and invaded the Middle East, Hungary, and Poland.

For all of his success, Ögödei had a major personal problem. He drank too much alcohol. He was so drunk toward the end of his life that he gave his wife, Toregene, the power to run the empire.[4] When Ögödei finally died in 1241, Toregene took the title of Great Empress, even though she wasn't a Mongol.

For the next ten years, there was a struggle for power. During most of that time, Toregene and other women were in control of the Mongol Empire. During this period, the empire did not expand. In fact, Mongol forces even pulled out of some territories. This situation happened because Genghis's other three sons had also died. One of Genghis's grandsons was then supposed to become the new Great Khan. The struggle came when the widows of each of Genghis Khan's dead sons pushed for one of their own sons to take over.

In 1246, Toregene's son Guyuk won the battle and became the next Great Khan. His rule didn't last long, however. He died less than two years later. After that, the struggle resumed. This gave some parts of the world a short breathing spell.

Finally in 1251, another grandson, Mongke, took over. He was a strong ruler. In 1257, Mongke Khan decided to take the Song Empire of southern China. To make sure the conquest went well, he sent his

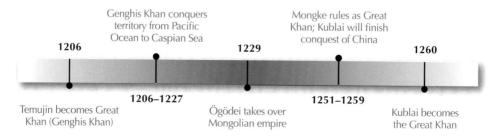

	Genghis Khan conquers territory from Pacific Ocean to Caspian Sea		Mongke rules as Great Khan; Kublai will finish conquest of China	
1206		**1229**		**1260**
	1206–1227		**1251–1259**	
Temujin becomes Great Khan (Genghis Khan)		Ögödei takes over Mongolian empire		Kublai becomes the Great Khan

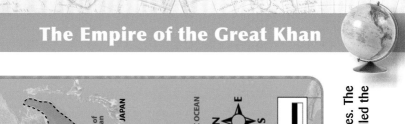

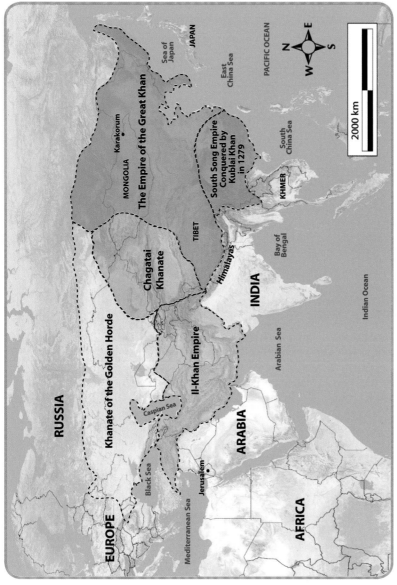

After the death of Genghis Khan, Genghis's four sons divided the vast empire among themselves. The most important section of those territories included most of present-day Mongolia and was called the Empire of the Great Khan.

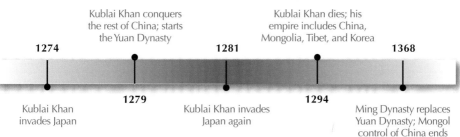

| 1274 | 1281 | 1368 |

Kublai Khan conquers the rest of China; starts the Yuan Dynasty

Kublai Khan dies; his empire includes China, Mongolia, Tibet, and Korea

| 1279 | 1294 |

Kublai Khan invades Japan

Kublai Khan invades Japan again

Ming Dynasty replaces Yuan Dynasty; Mongol control of China ends

Kublai Khan, grandson of Genghis Khan, finished the Mongol conquest of China. Then from his base in China, Kublai launched two unsuccessful sea invasions of Japan.

brother Kublai to lead the Mongol forces. Kublai pushed into Song territory, but Mongke died in 1259 before completion of that conquest.

Again, there was a rush for control of the Mongol Empire. In 1260, Kublai, supported by most of the Mongols, became the Great Khan. Some, however, favored his brother Arik-Boke. That set off a four-year civil war. Kublai won and remained in control until his death thirty-four years later.

As the Great Khan, Kublai took great interest in China. The north section was already his, but he wanted south China as well. To do this, he continued the invasion of the southern Song Empire he had begun when Mongke ruled.

Unlike his grandfather Genghis, however, Kublai realized that he could not conquer and hold all of China just by force.[5] Also unlike Genghis, Kublai Khan did care about the people in his empire. His rule was kinder, and he encouraged trade with all parts of the world. To show the Chinese that they should work with him instead of

Genghis Khan conquers
territory from Pacific
Ocean to Caspian Sea

Mongke rules as Great
Khan; Kublai will finish
conquest of China

1206　　　　　　　　**1229**　　　　　　　　**1260**

1206–1227　　　　　　**1251–1259**

Temujin becomes Great
Khan (Genghis Khan)

Ögödei takes over
Mongolian empire

Kublai becomes
the Great Khan

Italian adventurer Marco Polo kneels before Kublai Khan. Europe got its first real understanding about China from Marco Polo. He wrote marvelous stories about his travels and his stay in China.

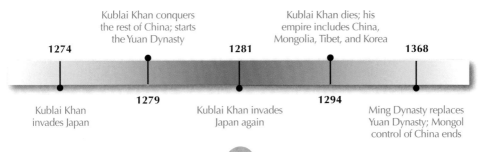

1274
Kublai Khan
invades Japan

1279

Kublai Khan conquers
the rest of China; starts
the Yuan Dynasty
1281
Kublai Khan invades
Japan again

Kublai Khan dies; his
empire includes China,
Mongolia, Tibet, and Korea
1294

1368
Ming Dynasty replaces
Yuan Dynasty; Mongol
control of China ends

fighting, he made many changes. We know about these changes and the way that Kublai governed because of Marco Polo, a famous Italian adventurer. Polo lived in China for many years during the time of Kublai Khan and wrote about his experiences.

Kublai moved the capital of his empire from Mongolia to the present-day capital of China, Beijing (bay-ZHING).[6] He wore Chinese clothes, used Chinese names, and even created his own Chinese Yuan Dynasty.

No matter how kind he tried to be, Kublai was still a conqueror. His desire was to expand his empire as much as he could in the shortest time possible. When people resisted, they lost their lives. By 1279, all of China was under Kublai's control. What had been a divided country with the biggest population in the world was now whole. From then on, it became the core of the Empire of the Great Khan. Kublai the conqueror even sent his forces as far south as present-day Vietnam, Myanmar (Burma), and Laos. In that manner, Chinese ways and people spread into Southeast Asia.

Genghis Khan looks out at the world from Mongolian money called tugrik. This 1,000 tugrik bill is worth close to one U.S. dollar. Genghis Khan is still so popular in Mongolia that his face or name appears everywhere.

However, when the Great Khan invaded by sea, it was a different story. He made two efforts to conquer Japan, in 1274 and 1281. He also sent an expedition to the island of Java in 1292. All three failed. He found that there were limits to his empire building.

At Kublai's death in 1294, the Empire of the Great Khan

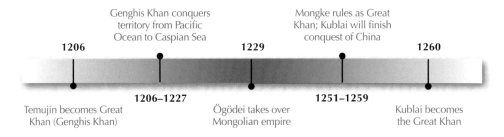

1206	1229	1260
	Genghis Khan conquers territory from Pacific Ocean to Caspian Sea	Mongke rules as Great Khan; Kublai will finish conquest of China

Temujin becomes Great Khan (Genghis Khan) — 1206–1227

Ögödei takes over Mongolian empire

1251–1259 — Kublai becomes the Great Khan

Modern-day horsemen in Mongolia compete during the Naadam festival. Mongolians have celebrated Naadam for centuries. For the first two days of the festival, athletes compete in horse racing, archery, and wrestling. Up to 1,000 horses may be chosen to compete. The third and final day is reserved for feasting and fun.

included China, Mongolia, Tibet, and Korea. Over the next 75 years, the power of the Great Khans slowly fell apart. In 1368, the Ming Dynasty of China finally took control of their country from the last of the Mongols. The Empire of the Great Khan was no more.

Even though Kublai Khan had unified their country, the Ming wanted to make sure that the Mongols never returned. To keep them

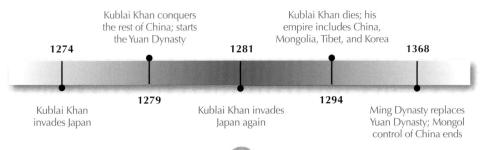

Kublai Khan conquers the rest of China; starts the Yuan Dynasty

Kublai Khan dies; his empire includes China, Mongolia, Tibet, and Korea

1274

1281

1368

1279

1294

Kublai Khan invades Japan

Kublai Khan invades Japan again

Ming Dynasty replaces Yuan Dynasty; Mongol control of China ends

The first Great Wall in China was made of compacted dirt during the Qin Dynasty. Many hundreds of years later, the Ming Dynasty created a new wall of the brick and stone we see today. The purpose of both walls was to keep out invading tribes like the Mongols.

out, they immediately began rebuilding the Great Wall of China with stone and brick.

In Mongolia today, most people see Genghis Khan as a national hero. Travelers who go to Mongolia find Genghis's picture or name everywhere. They simply have to look on the country's money, stamps, candy bars, and buildings. For Mongolians, Genghis Khan's conquests and the empire he began are a source of pride and great respect.[7]

Kublai Khan Meets the Divine Wind

In 1268, Kublai Khan decided that he wanted Japan as part of his empire. The problem was that the Japanese didn't agree. Not only that, his armies would have to cross the open sea to conquer Japan. The Mongols were great land fighters, but they knew very little about ships. To make up for this lack, Kublai turned to Chinese and Korean shipbuilders and sailors. It took a great deal of his wealth, but by 1274, Kublai's huge navy was ready. At that point, a Mongol army estimated at 40,000 men boarded 900 ships and set out for Japan.[8]

When they arrived on the northwestern coast of the Japanese island of Honshu, the Mongols quickly attacked and defeated the Japanese. The victory was clear but it didn't last long. A terrible storm, probably a typhoon, struck Kublai's fleet just as it was sailing for home. Hundreds of ships were lost and 13,000 men drowned.

Even with this loss, Kublai was sure the Japanese would now give up and become part of his empire. That didn't happen. Instead of surrendering, the Japanese cut off the heads of the people Kublai sent to negotiate in 1276.[9] That made Kublai furious.

Destruction of a Mongol invasion fleet by a kamikaze

Once again, the Great Khan set about building a huge navy. In 1281, he sent a reported 140,000 soldiers against the Japanese on 4,400 ships.[10] This time the Japanese were ready, and fighting raged for two months. Before a winner could be decided, a storm hit the invaders as they huddled aboard their ships. When nature's fury was over, 3,000 ships were missing along with 100,000 soldiers. Kublai never again tried to attack Japan.

Seeing two storms destroy two Mongol fleets left the Japanese feeling that their gods were protecting them. They even named the storms in honor of the gods, calling them *kamikaze* (kah-mih-KAH-zee), the Japanese word meaning "divine wind."

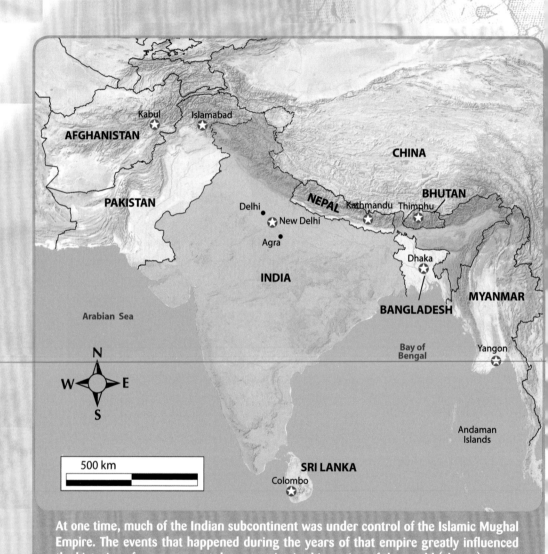

At one time, much of the Indian subcontinent was under control of the Islamic Mughal Empire. The events that happened during the years of that empire greatly influenced the histories of many present-day countries in this region of the world (shown).

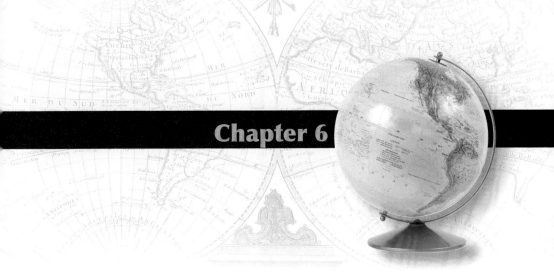

Chapter 6

The Mughal Empire

Babur "The Tiger" was tough and smart. This man with Mongol blood in his veins knew how to conquer. His family history included Genghis Khan and another great Mongol leader, Tamerlane. By the time of his death in 1530, Babur had given birth to the Mughal Empire that would last for two hundred years.

The people called the Mughals (MOO-gulls), like Babur, were what were left of the old Mongol Empire in Central Asia. The name Mughal was a Persian word that meant "Mongol." These Mongols were the ones who stayed in that region of the world after their empire broke apart in the fourteenth century. They also became Muslims, believers in the religion of Islam.

Babur didn't have a huge army, but he did have a secret weapon. That weapon was gunpowder. By using muskets and cannons, he was able conquer armies much bigger than his own. He began to create his empire in 1504 when he took Kabul in present-day Afghanistan. Then he crushed armies in north India. As Babur advanced on the cities of Agra and Dehli in 1526, his much smaller military force defeated an army of 100,000 men and 1,000 war elephants.[1] By the time of his death four years later, Babur had conquered Afghanistan and much of north India.

With Babur's death, the leadership of the empire fell upon Babur's son Humayun (hoo-MAW-yoon).* Humayun, however, didn't seem to care a great deal about running his empire. Instead, he spent much of

*Also transliterated as *Humanyun*.

Known as "The Tiger," Babur was the first Mughal emperor. His use of gunpowder allowed him to defeat armies much larger than his own.

his time studying astrology (using the stars to predict the future) and taking opium (an addictive drug).[2]

Without Babur's strong rule, the Mughal Empire quickly fell apart. The conquered territories rebelled and Mughal forces couldn't hold on to them. Within ten years, the empire was no more. In defeat, Humayun ran away to Persia. There he slowly rebuilt his armies and, over time, finally took back most of his empire. Before he was able to reclaim all of his lost lands, however, Humayun died. He met his death in 1556 by slipping and cracking his head on the stone steps of his observatory (a building created to observe the stars).[3]

Humayun's son Akbar stepped into his place, but he wasn't able to rule for a while. He was only thirteen years old. Other people ran the Mughal Empire until 1560. At that point, Akbar was old enough to take control and begin his own wars of conquest.

Akbar actually ruled the Mughal Empire for 45 years. During that time, he took back the rest of his father's lost territories and conquered all of North India. Like the Mongols of the past, Akbar preferred to

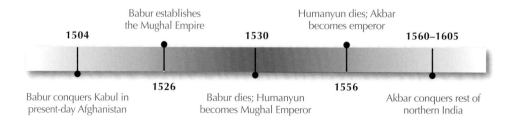

1504	Babur establishes the Mughal Empire 1530	Humanyun dies; Akbar becomes emperor 1560–1605
Babur conquers Kabul in present-day Afghanistan	1526 Babur dies; Humanyun becomes Mughal Emperor	1556 Akbar conquers rest of northern India

The tomb of Mughal Emperor Humayun, son of Babur. Humayun lost his father's empire and then regained much of it. He was buried in this tomb after he died by slipping and cracking his head on stone steps. His use of an addictive drug may have been a factor in his death.

take land and kingdoms without force if he could do it. When people resisted him, however, he had no mercy.

One group of rulers in 1567 found this out the hard way. Because they wouldn't surrender, Akbar personally led an attack on the fortress known as Chitor. When the fort was taken, 30,000 of Akbar's enemies were dead.[4]

As tough as he was, Akbar also knew how to get things done without violence. Instead of fighting, he often married the princesses of the

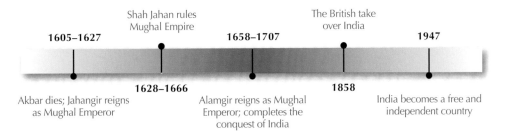

Shah Jahan rules Mughal Empire
1605–1627

The British take over India
1658–1707

1947

Akbar dies; Jahangir reigns as Mughal Emperor
1628–1666

Alamgir reigns as Mughal Emperor; completes the conquest of India
1858

India becomes a free and independent country

The Chitor (or Chittor) Fortress sits about 500 feet above the surrounding countryside in present-day Rajasthan, northwest India. Built in the seventh century CE, it covers about 700 acres and is encircled by a wall 8 miles long. The fort was attacked several times before Akbar and his soldiers looted and destroyed all the buildings in 1567.

kingdoms he wanted to conquer. In this way, he ended up with many wives and a great deal of territory without spilling blood.

In his wisdom, Akbar also made sure that all religions, not just Islam, were welcome in his empire. He proved this many times by inviting leaders of other faiths to discuss spiritual things with him in his palace.[5] Most of the people in India were Hindus and were very happy that they didn't have to become Muslims. Akbar was so interested in religion that he even made up his own, called "Divine Faith."

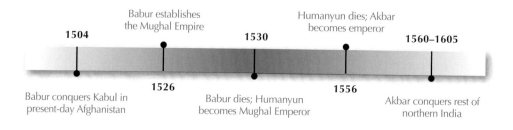

1504	Babur establishes the Mughal Empire	1530	Humanyun dies; Akbar becomes emperor	1560–1605
Babur conquers Kabul in present-day Afghanistan	1526	Babur dies; Humanyun becomes Mughal Emperor	1556	Akbar conquers rest of northern India

Not many people liked it, however. When he died, his religion died with him.

Government under Akbar was very well organized and set a pattern for the future. Hindus could now become part of that government along with Muslims and even join the empire's military. Akbar also commanded that his government treat the poor and the weak with fairness. Any officials who mistreated people received severe punishment. Akbar even got rid of a law that taxed people who were not Muslims, and he made the rich pay their fair share of the tax burden.

In the end, Akbar turned the Mughal Empire into one of the greatest in the Muslim world. He also became one of the most important rulers in Indian history.

Akbar ruled the Mughal Empire for forty-five years. Considered the greatest of the Mughal emperors, he continued to expand the empire. He also reformed the tax system; promoted commerce; encouraged science, literature, and the arts; and abolished slavery.

Upon Akbar's death in 1605, his favorite son[6], Salim, took over. Salim's new name as emperor became Jahangir (JHAN-ger), which meant "World-Conqueror." The new name was misleading. A "world-conqueror" he definitely was not. Jahangir did take over a few new parts of India but he also lost some territory there as well. Jahangir was

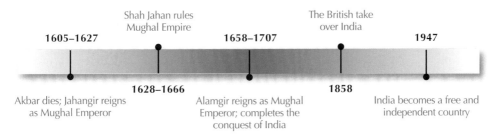

Shah Jahan rules Mughal Empire
1658–1707

The British take over India
1947

1605–1627

Akbar dies; Jahangir reigns as Mughal Emperor

1628–1666
Alamgir reigns as Mughal Emperor; completes the conquest of India

1858
India becomes a free and independent country

simply much more interested in things like art and architecture. Wine and opium also seemed more important to him than running his empire.[7]

Jahangir ruled for twenty-two years. When he died in 1627, his sons fought for power. One of them, Shah Jahan, became emperor the following year. Unlike his father, Shah Jahan took conquest more seriously. Under his rule for the next thirty years, much more of India became part of the Mughal Empire.

Very much like his father, Shah Jahan liked architecture. He seemed almost addicted to constructing buildings. Among his many architectural projects were the building of a new capital city, a huge palace, and a beautiful tomb for his wife after she died. All of that construction cost a great deal of money. The result was higher taxes. This made Shah Jahan unpopular, but he didn't care. His interest wasn't in making his people happy or even in making sure his government was doing a good job.

The Mughal Emperor Shah Jahan loved to have beautiful buildings constructed. One of the most well known was the Taj Mahal. This he built as a tomb for his dead wife.

Shah Jahan also liked to bully people, and it became a way of life in the empire. The emperor's

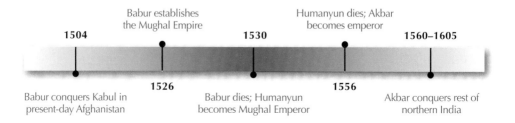

1504

Babur establishes the Mughal Empire

1530

Humanyun dies; Akbar becomes emperor

1560–1605

1526

1556

Babur conquers Kabul in present-day Afghanistan

Babur dies; Humanyun becomes Mughal Emperor

Akbar conquers rest of northern India

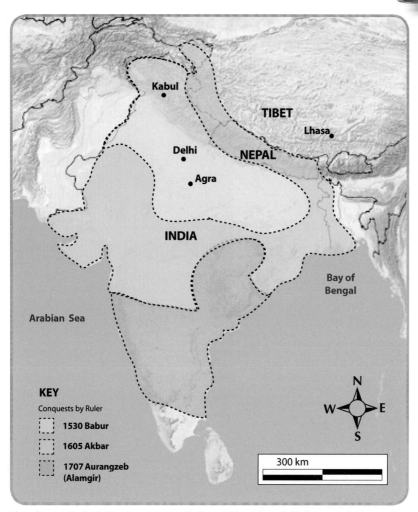

The first Mughal Emperor was Babur "The Tiger." Babur and five other generations of his family extended their rule over most of the Indian subcontinent. Shown here are the conquered territories by three of the greatest Mughal leaders.

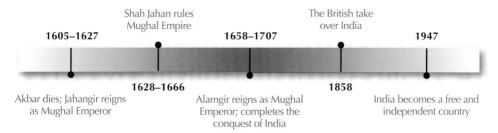

Shah Jahan rules Mughal Empire

1605–1627

The British take over India

1658–1707

1947

Akbar dies; Jahangir reigns as Mughal Emperor

1628–1666

Alamgir reigns as Mughal Emperor; completes the conquest of India

1858

India becomes a free and independent country

mean streak came back to haunt him when he became very sick in 1658. Expecting him to die, his four sons started fighting to take over the empire.

In a surprise to everyone, Shah Jahan suddenly recovered from his illness. The old emperor didn't enjoy his good health for long. Soon, his third son, Aurangzeb (OR-ang-zeb), captured Shah Jahan and threw him into prison. Aurangzeb immediately made himself emperor and went on to defeat his brothers. Shah Jahan lived out his life in prison, dying in 1666.

As did other emperors before him, Aurangzeb changed his name. He now called himself Alamgir, which means "Universe-Conqueror." The meaning of this name

The Amar Singh Gate of Agra Fort, the imperial city of the Mughal rulers. Inside its walls are the Jahangir Palace and the Khas Mahal (Private Palace), built by Shah Jahan; audience halls; and two very beautiful mosques. The fort is located across the Jamuna River from the Taj Mahal.

change was very important to him. It showed what the new emperor thought he was and would become. True to his new name, Emperor Alamgir attacked kingdom after kingdom. It took decades of brutal

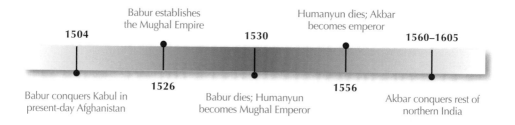

Babur establishes the Mughal Empire
1530

Humanyun dies; Akbar becomes emperor
1560–1605

1504

1526
Babur conquers Kabul in present-day Afghanistan

1556
Babur dies; Humanyun becomes Mughal Emperor

Akbar conquers rest of northern India

Aurangzeb, also known as Alamgir, was the last of the great Mughal emperors. He conquered a large piece of India down to its the southern tip and returned Islam as the central religion of his empire.

war, but when he was done, Alamgir was in control of almost all of India. Because of these wars, hundreds of thousands of lives were lost, as were great amounts of Mughal wealth. The human and material resources of the empire went to fund conquest.

Like his great-grandfather Akbar, Alamgir was a great conqueror. Unlike Akbar, however, he ruled the people of his empire with an iron hand. He also forced his belief in Islam on everyone else.[8] Islamic law became the law of the land. Hindus and believers of other religions had no choice but to do things Alamgir's way.

To pay for all his wars and for controlling his huge empire, Alamgir raised taxes on everyone. He even put back the hated tax on non-Muslims that Akbar had taken away. The Hindus of India now had to pay a tax just because they were Hindus.

Soon, starvation and disease swept through the empire. Many people were already angry with Alamgir, but now they blamed him for these new problems as well. Some of the old kingdoms rebelled against Mughal control.

Alamgir died in 1707. He would be the last of the great Mughal rulers. The empire began a long, slow death of its own.

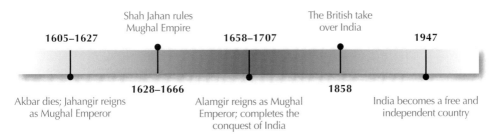

Shah Jahan rules Mughal Empire
1605–1627   1658–1707   The British take over India   1947
1628–1666   1858
Akbar dies; Jahangir reigns as Mughal Emperor   Alamgir reigns as Mughal Emperor; completes the conquest of India   India becomes a free and independent country

The Alamgiri Gate at Lahore Fort, built by Alamgir. The fort, which is in present-day Pakistan, is on the site of the first Mughal conquest of India. The city contains marble palaces and mosques decorated with mosaics and gold. The elegant gardens inside, including the magnificent Shalamar Gardens, contain waterfalls and fancy ponds.

The rebellions that had begun before his death continued. Over the next century and a half, the territories taken since the time of Babur "The Tiger" shrank to almost nothing. In 1858, the British took control of India and ended what little was left of the Mughal Empire. The people of India, who were unhappy with the British, finally drove them out in 1947. Modern India has become a free and independent country and is the largest democratic nation in the world.

Paradise on Earth

One of the most beautiful structures in the world is in northern India. The construction of this building complex began hundreds of years ago. Built mostly of white marble and red sandstone, it sits on the very edge of the Jamuna River and is known as the Taj Mahal.

It all started because of one simple word: love. In this case, it was the love of a man for a woman. The man was Shah Jahan, Mughal Emperor of India. Although he had many wives, his favorite was Mumtaz Mahal. When she died after bearing her fourteenth child in 1631, Shah Jahan was heartbroken. In honor of his lost love, the Emperor ordered the construction of the biggest and most lovely tomb imaginable. It took twenty years, 20,000 workers, and a great deal of the empire's wealth to complete. The Taj Mahal then became the final resting place of Mumtaz Mahal.

With its glistening marble, religious buildings, refreshing gardens, and cool reflecting pools, the Taj Mahal was Shah Jahan's idea of where one might go after death. The Emperor had deliberately created a tomb for his wife that looked like paradise on earth.[9]

Shah Jahan, however, didn't have long to enjoy his creation up close. In 1658, he became very sick and there was a fight for control of the Mughal Empire. Before he could fully recover, his son Aurangzeb threw him into prison and became Emperor. Shah Jahan spent the rest of his days living as a prisoner in the Agra fort directly across the Jamuna River from the Taj Mahal.[10] Perhaps he dreamed of his lost empire over the years as he gazed out his window and saw the white marble paradise he created.

India's Taj Mahal

Upon his death in 1666, he was entombed next to his beloved wife Mumtaz under the huge dome of the Taj Mahal.

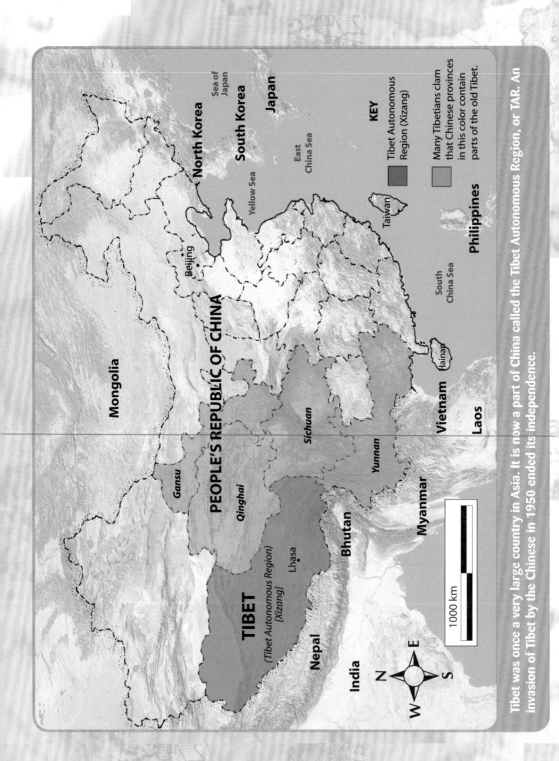

Tibet was once a very large country in Asia. It is now a part of China called the Tibet Autonomous Region, or TAR. An invasion of Tibet by the Chinese in 1950 ended its independence.

KEY

Tibet Autonomous Region (Xizang)

Many Tibetians clam that Chinese provinces in this color contain parts of the old Tibet.

Mongolia

PEOPLE'S REPUBLIC OF CHINA

Beijing

Gansu

Qinghai

Sichuan

Yunnan

TIBET
(Tibet Autonomous Region)
[Xizang]

Lhasa

Nepal

Bhutan

Myanmar

India

Laos

Vietnam

North Korea

South Korea

Japan

Sea of Japan

Yellow Sea

East China Sea

Taiwan

South China Sea

Hainan

Philippines

1000 km

N
W E
S

Tibet (Tibet Autonomous Region—TAR)

By 1965, the country of Tibet was no more. In the last half of the twentieth century, it disappeared from the maps of Asia. Now that land high in the mountains north of India is part of the People's Republic of China (PRC). This change was not a peaceful or a happy one for the Buddhist people of Tibet.

In 1950, the PRC invaded Tibet with 80,000 soldiers. It said that Tibet was just a runaway territory, a part of China. Now was the time, the PRC argued, to bring it back under the control of the PRC where it belonged.

In the past, Tibet had been under China's control to some degree, but it had also been a free country more than once. From the seventh through the tenth centuries, Tibet was independent. During those days, it even invaded China. Then up until the twentieth century, Tibet had mostly been under long-distance control by China but was generally left alone. When the PRC invaded in 1950, Tibet had again been a separate country since 1913.[1]

Tibet tried to resist the attack by the PRC. Its small army with old weapons fought bravely, but it was no match for so many well-armed Chinese troops. As PRC forces entered the country, they killed Tibetan citizens and spread terror. Chinese soldiers beheaded people, dragged them behind horses, and buried them alive.[2] Less than a year after the invasion, most of Tibet was firmly in the hands of the PRC. The end of its freedom came late in 1951 when 3,000 Chinese soldiers entered Lhasa, its capital.

Before 1960, the Potala Palace served as one of the Dalai Lama's homes. It also served as Tibet's main government building. Created starting in 1645 by the Fifth Dalai Lama, the palace has over 1,000 rooms.

The leader of Tibet at that time was a sixteen-year-old Buddhist monk named Tenzin Gyatso, and his title was Dalai Lama. Without getting the Dalai Lama's approval, the PRC had already forced a group of Tibetan leaders to agree that Tibet was part of China. The Chinese called the document signed by the Tibetans "The Seventeen-Point Agreement for the Peaceful Liberation of Tibet with China."

The takeover of a peace-loving and mostly nomadic people was almost complete. Over the next eight years, however, there was a fight

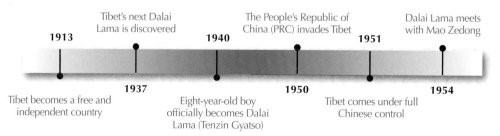

1913

Tibet's next Dalai Lama is discovered

1940

The People's Republic of China (PRC) invades Tibet

1951

Dalai Lama meets with Mao Zedong

1937
Tibet becomes a free and independent country

Eight-year-old boy officially becomes Dalai Lama (Tenzin Gyatso)

1950
Tibet comes under full Chinese control

1954

for the soul of Tibet. Even though the communist government of the PRC had no use for religion, it now controlled a country of very religious Buddhists.

With the world watching, the leaders of the PRC decided to allow the Dalai Lama to remain as Tibet's leader. In this way, they wanted to make the young monk their puppet. Their desire was to pull the strings and make the Dalai Lama do whatever they said. Then the PRC could always say that Tibetans and not the Chinese were running Tibet.

Leaving the young Dalai Lama as leader also kept peace with the people of

When he was sixteen years old, Tenzin Gyatso, the Fourteenth Dalai Lama of Tibet, faced a major crisis. As the religious and political leader of his country, he tried unsuccessfully to keep Tibet independent of China. For his efforts, he received the Nobel Peace Prize in 1989.

Tibet. To them, the Dalai Lama was almost a god-king. He was both head of the government and head of Tibet's Buddhist religion. If the PRC killed or even jailed the Dalai Lama, they would have had a great deal of trouble with Tibet's citizens.

The young Dalai Lama had little choice but to cooperate with the PRC. This he did. He hoped he could keep the peace and learn from

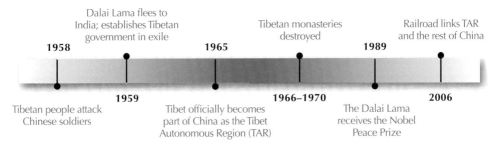

Dalai Lama flees to India; establishes Tibetan government in exile

1958

1959
Tibetan people attack Chinese soldiers

1965

Tibet officially becomes part of China as the Tibet Autonomous Region (TAR)

Tibetan monasteries destroyed

1966–1970

1989
The Dalai Lama receives the Nobel Peace Prize

Railroad links TAR and the rest of China

2006

the Chinese how to make his country more modern. His idea was to be positive and make the most out of a bad situation.

In a visit to China in 1954, the Dalai Lama met with the PRC leader, Mao Zedong, more than once. At one point, Mao instructed the young monk on how to run his country.[3] During another session, the Dalai Lama clearly saw how much Mao and the communists disliked religion. He realized that Buddhism in Tibet was in danger.

As time went on, the fiction of the Dalai Lama's power in Tibet wore thin. The PRC military in Tibet kept track of what the young monk did and said. PRC leaders also expected him to go along when they forced communist ways on Tibet's people.

Mao Zedong was the leader of China at the time of its invasion of Tibet in 1950. Mao believed that Tibet was just a backward runaway territory of China.

The PRC claimed that it wanted to help Tibet. However, it soon became obvious that the Chinese were stealing the country's wealth. Its soldiers raided Tibetan monasteries and homes of the rich. They also stepped up the beating, torturing, and execution of Tibet's citizens, including its monks.

By 1958, many of Tibet's people could stand the situation no longer. Some even organized and attacked the PRC military. Across Tibet, freedom fighters waged war. Both Tibetans and Chinese died in these

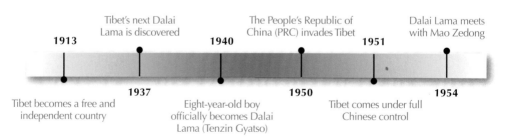

1913 — Tibet becomes a free and independent country

1937 — Tibet's next Dalai Lama is discovered

1940 — Eight-year-old boy officially becomes Dalai Lama (Tenzin Gyatso)

1950 — The People's Republic of China (PRC) invades Tibet

1951 — Tibet comes under full Chinese control

1954 — Dalai Lama meets with Mao Zedong

conflicts. The PRC then told the Dalai Lama to order his army to control the freedom fighters. When he refused, China sent more soldiers to Tibet. As the conflict continued into 1959, thousands of Tibetan people fled the fighting. Most of them went to Lhasa, more than doubling that city's population.

Being a man of peace and compassion, the Dalai Lama tried to stop both sides from killing each other. He hoped he could keep everyone calm, especially the Chinese. If he couldn't, he knew that many more people might die.

In March of 1959, the PRC military leaders in Lhasa invited the Dalai Lama to join them for entertainment at their headquarters. Not wanting to offend them, he accepted. Then the PRC commander said something very strange. He asked that the visit remain a secret as much as possible. Bring a few bodyguards with you, the commander told the Dalai Lama, but no soldiers.[4] All of this, he explained, was going to keep the Dalai Lama safe because he wouldn't attract as much attention.

Somehow, the people of Lhasa found out about this strange invitation. They were horrified. The Dalai Lama's people were sure the Chinese wanted to kidnap their much-loved leader. As the news spread like wildfire, people started gathering at the Dalai Lama's palace. They were going to protect their leader. Within a short time, an angry crowd of 30,000 people surrounded the palace and barricaded the streets. Many even started calling for the PRC to leave Tibet.

Fearing that the crowd might attack PRC soldiers, the Dalai Lama canceled his visit to the Chinese leaders. He hoped this would calm things down, but still the crowd refused to leave. This turn of events made the Chinese very unhappy. They demanded that the Dalai Lama

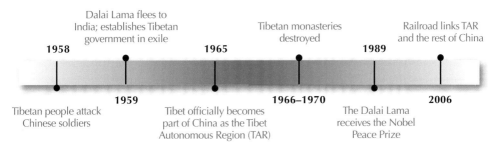

1958
Tibetan people attack
Chinese soldiers

1959

Dalai Lama flees to
India; establishes Tibetan
government in exile

1965
Tibet officially becomes
part of China as the Tibet
Autonomous Region (TAR)

1966–1970
Tibetan monasteries
destroyed

1989
The Dalai Lama
receives the Nobel
Peace Prize

2006
Railroad links TAR
and the rest of China

force the crowd to take down their barricades and then use his army to disarm the freedom fighters out in the countryside. The situation was getting out of control very quickly.

A few days later, just as the Dalai Lama's spiritual adviser was telling him that he should leave Tibet, two Chinese mortar shells exploded outside the palace near the huge crowd of people. It was then that the Dalai Lama knew he could no longer cooperate with the PRC. The only way to help his people, he decided, was to escape to India and set up his government there.

Under cover of darkness, the Dalai Lama secretly left the palace. Along with his family and advisers, he began a long and difficult trip by horseback across the mountains to India. Escorted by 350 Tibetan soldiers and freedom fighters, the Dalai Lama and his group took two weeks to reach safety.

Within 48 hours of the Dalai Lama's departure, the Chinese attacked his palace and the crowd around it. Using mortars and machine guns, they killed 3,000 people.[5] The iron hand of PRC control had begun to close into a fist.

In 1965, Tibet officially became part of China. Its new name from then on was the Tibet Autonomous Region, or TAR. The PRC used the word *autonomous* to show the world that Tibet still had a great deal of freedom. *Autonomous* means to exist without control by others.

The reality of the situation, however, soon became very clear. In the period from 1966 to 1970, the Chinese made a major effort to wipe out Tibet's Buddhist religion and culture. The result was the destruction of 6,000 monasteries and holy places.[6] Many Buddhist monks and nuns either went to prison or were killed.

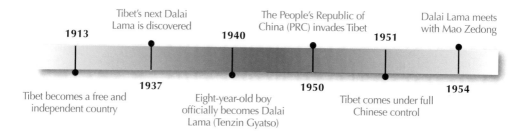

Tibet's next Dalai Lama is discovered

The People's Republic of China (PRC) invades Tibet

Dalai Lama meets with Mao Zedong

1913   1940   1951

1937   1950   1954

Tibet becomes a free and independent country

Eight-year-old boy officially becomes Dalai Lama (Tenzin Gyatso)

Tibet comes under full Chinese control

Buddhism has been the religion of Tibet's people for well over a thousand years. These Tibetan Buddhist monks are followers of Tenzin Gyatso, the Fourteenth Dalai Lama.

In the years since those terrible days, many thousands of Chinese people from the PRC have moved into the former country of Tibet. In 2006, a new railroad over the mountains directly connected China with its Tibet Autonomous Region (TAR).[7] In China, the TAR has become something like a province or state. It even has a different name: Xizang (she-ZANG).

Many Tibetan people, however, say that the Chinese maps showing the TAR as all of old Tibet are wrong. To them, old Tibet also

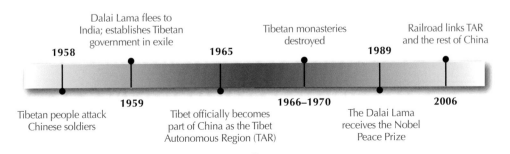

1958		1965		1989	
Dalai Lama flees to India; establishes Tibetan government in exile			Tibetan monasteries destroyed		Railroad links TAR and the rest of China

1959 — Tibetan people attack Chinese soldiers

1966–1970 — Tibet officially becomes part of China as the Tibet Autonomous Region (TAR)

The Dalai Lama receives the Nobel Peace Prize

2006

In 2006, a railway between China and the TAR opened to the public. In traveling to Tibet, this train travels high across mountains and plateaus. Because it reaches altitudes of over three miles above sea level, the railway provides oxygen to the passengers.

included parts of the present-day Chinese provinces of Qinghai, Gansu, Yunnan, and Sichuan.[8]

To this day, the Dalai Lama lives in Dharamsala, India, where he set up his government in exile back in 1959. In 1989, the Dalai Lama accepted the Nobel Peace Prize for his struggle to free Tibet in nonviolent ways. The thousands of Tibetans who left their country after the Dalai Lama fled still consider him their spiritual and political leader. Together, they hope that someday they might be able to return to a Tibet free of China's iron grip.

The Search for a New Dalai Lama

When the Thirteenth Dalai Lama died in 1933, Tibet had to find a new leader. The Buddhists of Tibet have always believed that their Dalai Lamas share the same spirit.[9] For them, the death of the Dalai Lama simply meant that his spirit was to be reborn into a young child. The problem then was to find that child. They had specific rules to follow in making the search. This took a great deal of time and effort.

Tibet's Thirteenth Dalai Lama

In 1937, search teams began looking for the new Dalai Lama. In the meantime, Tibet had appointed a temporary leader. To find the right child, the search teams used the secret details of a spiritual vision by the temporary leader.

When one team found a house matching the vision, they asked to stay the night. The team also said nothing about why they were there. Once inside the house, the leader of the search team realized that the two-year-old boy living there might truly be the one they were looking for.

The search party's leader hid rosary beads belonging to the dead Dalai Lama inside his robes. The child found them anyway and immediately said they were his.[10] The boy also knew the leader's name, even though no one had told him.

When the search party then tested the child using other belongings of the Thirteenth Dalai Lama, he was correct each time. As he identified an item, he also told them, "It's mine."[11] With such strong evidence, the search party agreed they had found the right child. In 1940 at age five, the boy became the Fourteenth Dalai Lama with a new name: Tenzin Gyatso.

This Dalai Lama would be the last to rule Tibet before it became the Tibet Autonomous Region of China.

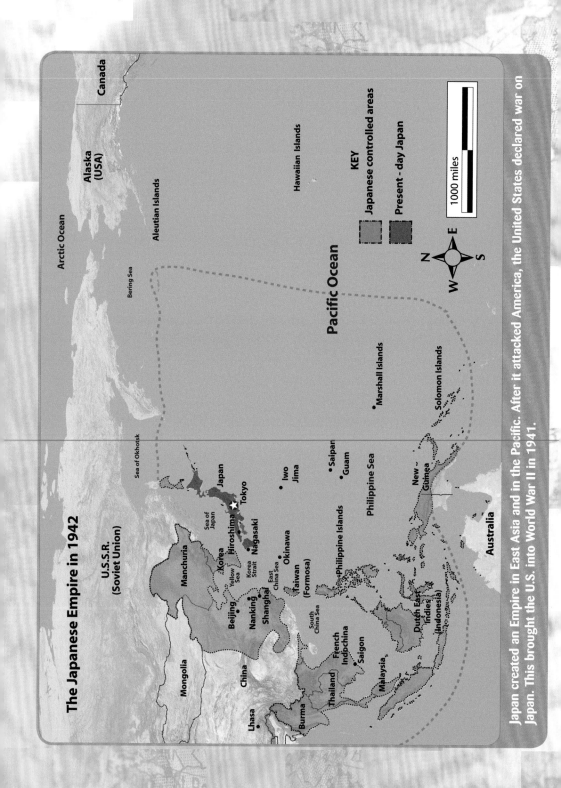

The Japanese Empire in 1942

U.S.S.R.
(Soviet Union)

Mongolia

Manchuria

China

Lhasa

Burma

Thailand

French Indochina

Saigon

Malaysia

Beijing

Nanking

Shanghai

Korea

Korea Strait

Yellow Sea

East China Sea

South China Sea

Dutch East Indies (Indonesia)

Taiwan (Formosa)

Philippine Islands

Okinawa

Hiroshima

Nagasaki

Sea of Japan

Japan

Tokyo

Iwo Jima

Saipan

Guam

Philippine Sea

New Guinea

Australia

Sea of Okhotsk

Bering Sea

Arctic Ocean

Sea of Japan

Aleutian Islands

Alaska (USA)

Canada

Pacific Ocean

Marshall Islands

Solomon Islands

Hawaiian Islands

KEY

Japanese controlled areas

Present - day Japan

N E S W

1000 miles

Japan created an Empire in East Asia and in the Pacific. After it attacked America, the United States declared war on Japan. This brought the U.S. into World War II in 1941.

The Empire of Japan

On December 7, 1941, Japan attacked the United States at Pearl Harbor, Hawaii. It was a bold move. The idea was to destroy American naval forces in the Pacific. With U.S. ships out of the way, Japanese leaders hoped, the Empire of Japan could continue to expand.[1]

The attack that day came without warning from nearby Japanese aircraft carriers. Planes from those ships sank or damaged eight U.S. battleships, a dozen other vessels, and nearly 200 airplanes. The number of American military people killed or wounded stood at close to 4,000.[2] As unprepared as it was to strike back, the United States declared war on Japan and entered World War II on the following day.

By early 1942, the Empire of Japan covered a large portion of the earth's surface.[3] To much of the world, the Japanese war machine seemed unstoppable. Many Americans even feared a Pacific coast invasion.

Japan's rise to such strength had happened over the very short period of less than fifty years. In the late nineteenth century, Japan saw non-Asian countries in control of Asian territory. Among these were the United States, France, the United Kingdom, the Netherlands, and Russia (later the Soviet Union). Fearful of losing all or part of its lands to these non-Asian countries, Japan built up its military and even began taking control of its share of non-Japanese territory.

Japan's move toward creating an empire got under way after it gained control of the island of Formosa in 1895, following its one-

Chapter 8

sided victory in a war with China. Then when Japan beat Russia in the Russo-Japanese War of 1905, it truly became a world power. Five years later, Japan officially made Korea part of the Japanese Empire. In World War I, Japan took control of the Caroline, Mariana, and Marshall island groups in the Pacific.[4]

The full march toward an even bigger empire for Japan, however, began with money trouble across the globe. An economic depression that started in the United States had become worldwide. Like other countries, Japan faced hard times starting in 1929.

It was in that year and in the early 1930s that businesses closed, exports fell, and jobs became scarce. This forced the Japanese to look closely at their government,

Emperor Hirohito of Japan visited the U.S. after World War II in 1975. During that visit, he met the movie actor John Wayne and President Gerald Ford. Hirohito even picked up a Mickey Mouse watch while in the U.S and wore it for many years.

their resources, and their industries. They did not like what they saw. Much of Japan's imports came from the United States. This included most of its fuel needs. For a proud and independent people, this situation had to change.

Into this situation marched the Japanese military. They saw their elected government as too weak to solve their country's problems, and

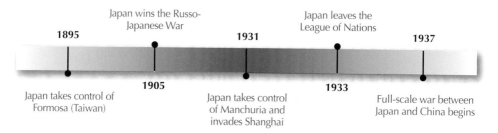

Japan wins the Russo-Japanese War

1895

1931

Japan leaves the League of Nations

1937

1905

Japan takes control of Formosa (Taiwan)

1933

Japan takes control of Manchuria and invades Shanghai

Full-scale war between Japan and China begins

Japan's emperor, Hirohito, had very limited power. They were also sure there would someday be war with the United States and the Soviet Union. Without strong rulers, they felt, Japan would be at risk.

To make things happen their way, Japan's military leaders pushed their government toward creating a greatly expanded empire. In time, they would actually become the rulers of their country and try to con-

quer as much of Asia as possible. This, they were sure, was the only way to truly protect Japan and make it a great country. The country's weak emperor, Hirohito, supported the military leaders.

Japan's push for an even larger empire began in 1931 when its army invaded the northern Chinese territory of Manchuria. Manchuria then served as a protective barrier between Japan and the Soviet Union. It also provided Japan with much-needed raw materials like iron and coal.

Soon after that, Japan attacked the Chinese city of Shanghai. Japan claimed it was protecting Japanese citizens living in Shanghai, as

Japanese soldiers in Shanghai, 1937. Japan was criticized by the League of Nations for an attack on Shanghai and on Manchuria. In response, Japan gave up its membership in the League.

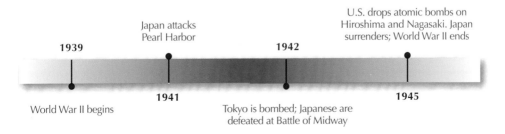

1939
World War II begins

Japan attacks
Pearl Harbor
1941

1942
Tokyo is bombed; Japanese are
defeated at Battle of Midway

U.S. drops atomic bombs on
Hiroshima and Nagasaki. Japan
surrenders; World War II ends
1945

well as the property of those citizens. However, when China protested these two invasions to the League of Nations, an international organization dedicated to world peace, the League criticized Japan. To most of the world, Japan was clearly in the wrong. The Japanese response was to give up their League membership. They didn't care what the world thought.

In 1937, all-out war between China and Japan began. The Japanese bombed Shanghai, captured Beijing, and crushed Nanking. The treatment of people in Nanking and other cities in China by the invaders was horrible and bloody beyond belief. Japanese soldiers set people on fire, bayoneted pregnant women, and forced children into minefields.[5] A final count of Chinese soldiers and civilians killed in Nanking alone was close to 300,000. A special Japanese military unit even did experiments with diseases, using human beings as guinea pigs.[6]

As the war in China dragged on, the United States began to see Japan as a real threat in the Pacific. In 1940, after Japan moved into Southeast Asia, the U.S. stopped selling aviation fuel and scrap metal to Japan.

Also in 1940, the Japanese decided they needed some friends in the world to help protect them in case of war. The result was a treaty with Nazi (NOT-zee) Germany and Fascist (FAA-shist) Italy. World War II had already begun in Europe, but it would soon include Asia as well.

When U.S. President Franklin D. Roosevelt finally stopped selling oil to Japan, the Japanese felt strangled. Without oil, they would not be able to expand or maybe even keep their empire.

Japan wins the Russo-Japanese War
1895
1931
Japan leaves the League of Nations
1937
Japan takes control of Formosa (Taiwan)
1905
Japan takes control of Manchuria and invades Shanghai
1933
Full-scale war between Japan and China begins

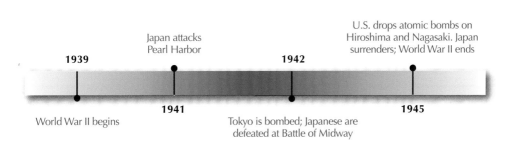

On December 7, 1941, Japan attacked the United States at Pearl Harbor, Hawaii. On that day, Japanese airplanes sank or damaged eight U.S. battleships, a dozen other vessels, and 200 airplanes. The number of killed or wounded Americans stood close to 4,000.

The new military leader of Japan, General Tojo, concluded that he must attack the United States. The strike at Pearl Harbor in 1941 was his attempt to cripple the United States and free Japan from any U.S. control. In response to the Pearl Harbor attack, the United States declared war on Japan. This brought both countries fully into World War II. The Japanese called their part in the conflict the Great Eastern Asia War.

1939		Japan attacks Pearl Harbor		1942		U.S. drops atomic bombs on Hiroshima and Nagasaki. Japan surrenders; World War II ends

World War II begins   1941   Tokyo is bombed; Japanese are defeated at Battle of Midway   1945

The American loss of life and ships at Pearl Harbor hurt the United States but not as badly as Japan had hoped. It did give the Japanese time to conquer more territory. The Pearl Harbor attack also convinced people in the United States that whether they wanted to go to war or not, they had to fight the Japanese. Up until that point, many Americans felt that the U.S. should stay out of the problems Japan was causing in Asia.

By early 1942, the Japanese had taken Singapore, the Philippines, the Dutch East Indies (modern-day Indonesia), Burma, and other territory. They even captured two islands in Alaska's Aleutian Island chain in early June of that year.

In those days when the Empire of Japan was at its highest point, the tide of battle started to change. In April of 1942, U.S. Lieutenant Colonel Jimmy Doolittle led a bombing raid on Tokyo, Japan's capital. Taking off from a U.S. aircraft carrier 600 miles from Japan, the Doolittle Raiders delivered a message from the United States to the Japanese: "Look out! Here we come!" Less than two months later, the U.S. Navy defeated the Japanese at the Battle of Midway. Japan would never recover from losing four aircraft carriers in that battle.

By 1943, with U.S. factories producing huge amounts of war supplies, American military and naval forces began a full push toward Japan. In less than two years, the American war machine would take key Japanese-held island chains in the Pacific. The U.S. called it "island hopping," but it was brutal, ugly fighting. Many thousands of soldiers died on each side.

In the spring of 1945, World War II in Europe finally ended. With Germany and Italy defeated, the United States was free to focus all its might on its enemy in the Pacific. Hoping to break the will of the Japa-

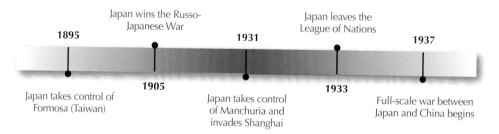

Japan wins the Russo-Japanese War
1895
1931
Japan leaves the League of Nations
1937

Japan takes control of Formosa (Taiwan)
1905
Japan takes control of Manchuria and invades Shanghai
1933
Full-scale war between Japan and China begins

The Doolittle Raiders from left to right: Staff Sergeant Paul J. Leonard, flight engineer/gunner; Lieutenant Richard E. Cole, copilot; Staff Sergeant Fred A. Braemer, bombardier; Lieutenant Colonel James H. Doolittle, pilot and mission commander; and Lieutenant Henry A. Potter, navigator.

nese, the United States began firebombing Japanese cities. The attacks created intense firestorms, especially in Tokyo. Hundreds of thousands of people either died in these bombings or suffered horrible injuries.[7]

This didn't discourage the Japanese, it just made them very angry. Instead of thinking about surrender, they prepared to fight the Americans in any way they could. The leaders of Japan even had their pilots

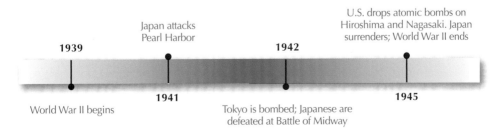

1939

World War II begins

1941

Japan attacks
Pearl Harbor

1942

Tokyo is bombed; Japanese are
defeated at Battle of Midway

U.S. drops atomic bombs on
Hiroshima and Nagasaki. Japan
surrenders; World War II ends

1945

fly airplanes directly into U.S. ships. These were suicide flights, final efforts to halt the advance of the U.S. Navy. The Japanese name for these attacks was *Kamikaze,* or Divine Wind.

As the United States made plans to invade Japan, it became clear that this final part of the war would cost many lives. The U.S. was confident that Japan would lose, but it would be a long and bloody effort. U.S. military experts predicted one million dead and wounded American soldiers.[8] The loss to the Japanese would be many millions more.

Led by Lieutenant Colonel Jimmy Doolittle, a U.S. Army B-25 Mitchell bomber takes off from the deck of the USS *Hornet* in the Pacific Ocean. The bomber is on its way to take part in first U.S. air raid on Japan, April 18, 1942.

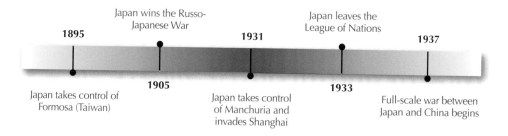

1895

Japan takes control of Formosa (Taiwan)

1905

Japan wins the Russo-Japanese War

1931

Japan takes control of Manchuria and invades Shanghai

1933

Japan leaves the League of Nations

1937

Full-scale war between Japan and China begins

Then America's new president, Harry Truman, made a decision that would change the world forever. Instead of invading Japan, he ordered the U.S. military to drop a new type of bomb on the Japanese city of Hiroshima. He hoped this atomic bomb, as American scientists called it, would end the war quickly.

When the American atomic bomb exploded over Hiroshima, it destroyed the central part of the city. Over 100,000 people died. The

General Tojo Hideki, second from left, sits with other high-ranking Japanese people awaiting trial after the war. Tojo was head of Japan's government during most of World War II. He was convicted of war crimes and executed in 1948.

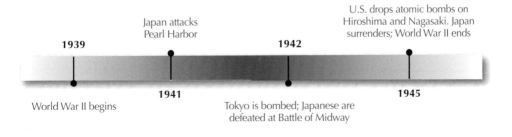

U.S. drops atomic bombs on Hiroshima and Nagasaki. Japan surrenders; World War II ends

Japan attacks Pearl Harbor

1939

1942

1941

1945

World War II begins

Tokyo is bombed; Japanese are defeated at Battle of Midway

world had never seen such destruction. Still the Japanese military leaders would not give up. The United States then dropped another atomic bomb, this one on Nagasaki. With the destruction of that city, the Japanese government finally decided to surrender. The Empire of Japan that had caused the deaths of at least 10 million Asian people was no more. With that surrender, World War II came an end.

After that terrible conflict, just as it did with Germany and Italy, the United States helped Japan rebuild its cities and its society. Slowly a great democratic nation of peace and wealth rose out of the ruins of war. Japan now trades with countries around the globe instead of fighting for what it wants. The once-feared Japanese military exists today only to defend Japan from attack.

After the atomic bomb exploded over Nagasaki on August 9, 1945, a mushroom cloud rose ten miles high over the city. An estimated 40,000 people were killed instantly, and about 25,000 were injured. Many thousands more would die later from related injuries and radiation sickness.

Hiroshima

On the sunny morning of August 6, 1945, the people of Hiroshima had just begun their daily activities. Traffic filled the streets, and those who saw the lone airplane high above didn't worry. Fear would only come if the sky became filled with American warplanes. One aircraft, they thought, would be no threat.

That one aircraft, however, was an American B-29 bomber with a special load. In its belly lay a single bomb with an explosive force equal to 20,000 tons of TNT. The United States called it an "atomic bomb" because it could unleash the power of the atom. U.S. leaders hoped that dropping it on Hiroshima would convince the Japanese to surrender.

The bomb "Little Boy" was dropped on Hiroshima.

At exactly 8:15 A.M., the B-29 released its load. The bomb dropped for forty-three seconds before exploding in midair. In that instant, a blinding fireball bloomed with a temperature of 7,000 degrees Fahrenheit. It blasted away the heart of Hiroshima.

Nearly every building within a mile of the explosion's center was destroyed.[9] The tremendous heat melted steel, caused flying birds to burst into flame, and burned human beings into nothingness. Two miles away from the blast's center, telephone poles were scorched on one side. Small fires erupted all around the city and then merged into one huge firestorm. A towering cloud of smoke, dust, and blasted material rose high above Hiroshima.

Horribly burned and badly cut, many survivors quickly sickened and died. Others without faces, with eyes burned away,[10] or with skin hanging from their bodies cried out for help that rarely came.

Years later, many survivors were still dying of illnesses caused by the bomb's radiation. An estimate of bomb-related deaths by 1950—five years after the blast—put the number at more than 200,000.[11]

Hiroshima aftermath

Timeline

BCE

475–221	The "Warring States Period" of Chinese history.
247	Thirteen-year-old Ying Zheng becomes king of Qin.
230	Ying Zheng begins fight to control remaining Warring States.
221	Ying Zheng of Qin completes conquest of the Warring States, creates an empire and calls himself Qin Shi Huangdi ("The First Emperor").
213	Qin Shi Huangdi orders the burning of all but specially selected books.
212	Qin Shi Huangdi orders 460 scholars buried alive.
210	Qin Shi Huangdi dies.
206	The Han Dynasty takes over China and rules for over 400 years.

CE

1206–1227	Genghis Khan conquers huge amounts of territory from the Pacific Ocean to the Caspian Sea.
1206	Great Assembly of Mongolian tribesmen declares Temujin as Great Khan; he takes name Genghis Khan.
1229	Genghis Khan's son Ögödei takes over Mongolian empire two years after Genghis's death and expands it.
1251–1259	Mongke rules as Great Khan and sends Kublai to finish conquest of China.
1260	Kublai, the grandson of Genghis Khan, becomes the Great Khan.
1274	Kublai Khan invades Japan for the first time and fails.
1279	Kublai Khan conquers the rest of China and starts the Yuan Dynasty.
1281	Kublai Khan invades Japan and again fails to conquer it.
1294	Kublai Khan dies; his empire includes China, Mongolia, Tibet, and Korea.
1368	Ming Dynasty replaces the Yuan Dynasty and control of China by the Mongols ends.
1504	Babur "The Tiger" comes out of central Asia and conquers Kabul in present-day Afghanistan.

Timeline

1526	Babur conquers much of northern India and establishes the Mughal Empire.
1530	Babur dies; Humanyun becomes Mughal Emperor.
1556	Humanyun dies; Akbar becomes Mughal Emperor.
1560	Akbar conquers the rest of northern India and establishes excellence in his government.
1605	Akbar dies; Jahangir becomes as Mughal Emperor and reigns until 1627.
1628	Shah Jahan takes over the Mughal Empire and reigns until 1658.
1658–1707	Alamgir reigns as Mughal Emperor and completes the conquest of India. He is the last of the Great Mughals.
1858	The British take over India.
1895	Japan takes control of the island of Formosa (Taiwan) after war with China.
1905	Japan wins the Russo-Japanese War and becomes a world power.
1913	Tibet becomes a free and independent country.
1931	Japan takes control of Manchuria and lands soldiers in Shanghai, both Chinese territories.
1933	Japan leaves the League of Nations after being criticized for taking territory in China.
1937	Tibet's next Dalai Lama, a five-year-old boy, is discovered. Three years later, the boy officially becomes the next Dalai Lama with the name Tenzin Gyatso. Full-scale war begins between Japan and China as Japan invades more Chinese territory.
1939	World War II begins in Europe.
1940	Japan becomes allied with Nazi Germany and Fascist Italy.
1941	Japan attacks the United States at Pearl Harbor on December 7.
1942	Doolittle bombers raid Tokyo; Japan is badly defeated by U.S. naval forces at the Battle of Midway, which turns the tide of war against Japan.
1945	U.S. drops atomic bombs on Hiroshima and Nagasaki. Japan surrenders. World War II is officially over.

1947	India becomes a free and independent country.
1948	Burma becomes a free and independent country, with democratic elections.
1950	The People's Republic of China (PRC) invades Tibet.
1951	Tibet comes under full Chinese control.
1953	Cambodia becomes a free and independent country.
1954	Vietnam splits into North Vietnam and South Vietnam. Tibet's young Dalai Lama goes to China and meets with Mao Zedong.
1955	South Vietnam becomes the Republic of South Vietnam.
1956	Supported by North Vietnam, guerrilla warfare against South Vietnam begins.
1958	Tibetan people attack Chinese soldiers in Tibet.
1959	Dalai Lama flees to India and establishes Tibetan government in exile.
1961	U.S. President John F. Kennedy sends military advisers to South Vietnam.
1962	Ne Win and other generals take over Burma, abolishing elections.
1965	U.S. President Lyndon B. Johnson commits U.S. military to fight Vietnamese communists. Tibet officially becomes part of China as the Tibet Autonomous Region (TAR).
1966–1970	Chinese communists destroy Tibetan monasteries and attack Tibetan people.
1969	The United States begins bombing campaign against North Vietnamese troops in Cambodia.
1970	General Lon Nol takes leadership of Cambodia and changes name to Khmer Republic; civil war begins.
1973	U.S. President Richard Nixon makes peace with North Vietnam; U.S. troops withdraw. United States ends bombing campaign in Cambodia.
1974	A new constitution allows Burmese military to remain in control; the country is renamed Socialist Republic of Burma. Qin Shi Huangdi's underground terra-cotta army is discovered.
1975	North Vietnamese forces capture Saigon and the rest of South Vietnam. The civil war in Cambodia ends; Pol Pot and the Red

	Khmers take control of Cambodia and change the name to Democratic Kampuchea.
1976	North and South Vietnam officially unite as the Socialist Republic of Vietnam; Saigon becomes Ho Chi Minh City.
1979	Vietnamese invade Cambodia and take control from Red Khmers; they change name to People's Republic of Kampuchea.
1988	Widespread protests in Burma; formation of State Law and Order Council in Burma; Aung San Suu Kyi returns to Burma and speaks out against the military.
1989	Vietnamese leave Cambodia. Burma is renamed Myanmar; Aung San Suu Kyi is placed under house arrest. The Dalai Lama receives the Nobel Peace Prize.
1990	Aung San Suu Kyi's NLD party wins the election in Myanmar but Myanmar's generals prevent them from taking power.
1991	Aung San Suu Kyi receives Nobel Peace Prize.
1993	Cambodia becomes the Kingdom of Cambodia.
1995	U.S. President Bill Clinton establishes normal diplomatic relations with Vietnam.
1998	Former Red Khmer leader Pol Pot dies.
2006	International judges are sworn in to put any Red Khmers still alive on trial. Aung San Suu Kyi's house arrest is extended again. A new railroad line links Tibet (TAR) and the rest of China.
2007	China tests an anti-satellite missile. The United States and Japan form an alliance in response to the buildup of nuclear weapons in North Korea.

Chapter Notes

Chapter 1. Saigon (Ho Chi Minh City)

1. David Butler, *The Fall of Saigon* (New York: Simon & Schuster, 1985), p. 19.
2. Stanley Karnow, *Vietnam: A History* (New York: Viking Press, 1983), p. 204.
3. Butler, p. 119.
4. Ibid., pp. 164–165.
5. Ibid., p. 380.
6. Kirsten Scharnberg, "Last One to Leave and Frantic Last Mission With Ambassador," *Fall of Saigon Marine Association*, April 30, 2005, http://www.fallofsaigon.org/lastoleave_frantic_mission.htm
7. George Esper, *ABC News*: "Fall of Saigon Remembered Anew," April 28, 2005, http://abcnews.go.com/International/print?id=710508
8. Butler, p. 458.
9. Ibid., p. 460.
10. CNN.com: "Vietnam Marks Fall of Saigon," April 30, 2005, http://www.cnn.com/2005/WORLD/asiapcf/04/30/vietnam.anniversary
11. Jennifer Loven, "Bush Compares U.S. Wars in Vietnam, Iraq," *U.S. News and World Report*, November 17, 2006, http://www.redorbit.com/news/general/734999/bush_compares_us_wars_in_vietnam_iraq/index.html
12. Stanley Karnow, TIME 100: Ho Chi Minh, "He married nationalism to communism and perfected the deadly art of guerilla warfare," http://www.time.com/time/time100/leaders/profile/hochiminh.html
13. William J. Duiker, *Ho Chi Minh: A Life* (New York: Hyperion, 2000), p. 566.
14. New York Times Travel Guides: Hanoi, "Ho Chi Minh's Mausoleum," http://travel.nytimes.com/travel/guides/asia/vietnam/hanoi/attraction-detail.html?vid=1154654613651&inline=nyt-classifier

Chapter 2. Kampuchea (Cambodia)

1. David Chandler, *A History of Cambodia* (Sydney: Allen & Unwin, 1992), p. 212.
2. Ibid., p. 228.
3. Ibid., p. 209.
4. Ibid., p. 213.
5. Ibid., p. 209.
6. David Chandler, *The Tragedy of Cambodian History: Politics, War and Revolution Since 1945* (New Haven, CT, Yale University Press, 1991), p. 241.
7. Ibid., p. 249.
8. Chandler, *A History of Cambodia*, p. 225.
9. "A Brief History of Our Kingdom," Ministry of Tourism, Cambodia Home of World Heritage, http://www.mot.gov.kh/history.asp

Chapter 3. Burma (Myanmar)

1. Mary Somers Heidhues, *Southeast Asia: A Concise History* (London: Thames & Hudson, 2000), p. 177.

2. Barbara Victor, *The Lady: Aung San Suu Kyi: Nobel Laureate and Burma's Prisoner* (Boston: Farber & Farber, 1998), p. 1.

3. Ibid., p. 40.

4. Ibid., p. 56.

5. Ibid., p. 85.

6. Aung San Suu Kyi, *Freedom From Fear and Other Writings* (London, Penguin, 1995), p. 309.

7. "Suu Kyi's Detention Extended, Supporters Likely to Protest," *The Irrawaddy News Magazine Online Edition*, May 27, 2006, http://www.Irrawaddy.org/aviewer. asp?a=5797&z=154

8. Victor, p. 7.

9. Aung San Suu Kyi, p. 309.

10. Victor, p. 88.

Chapter 4. The Qin Empire (China)

1. Patricia Buckley Ebrey, *Cambridge Illustrated History of China* (London: Cambridge University Press, 1996), p. 61.

2. Ibid., p. 82.

3. Minnesota State University, Mankato, Emuseum, "Qin Dynasty," http://www. mnsu.edu/emuseum/prehistory/china/early_imperial_china/qin.html

4. Ray Huang, *China: A Macro History* (London: M.E. Sharpe, Inc., 1990), p. 30.

5. Ebrey, p. 63.

6. Huang, p. 28.

7. Ibid., p. 32.

8. O. Louis Mazzatenta, "China's Warriors Rise From the Earth," *National Geographic*, October 1996, pp. 69–85.

9. "The Mausoleum of Qin Shi Huangdi," University of Texas at Austin, http:// www.utexas.edu/courses/wilson/ant304/biography/arybios98/smithbio.html

10. Emperor Qin's Terra-Cotta Warriors and Horses Museum, http://211.147.225.34/gate/big5/www.bmy.com.cn/english/bwgjs/l2p.htm

11. "The Mausoleum of Qin Shi Huangdi."

Chapter 5. The Empire of the Great Khan

1. University of Pennsylvania Museum of Archaeology and Anthropology, "Modern Mongolia: Reclaiming Genghis Khan," http://www.museum.upenn.edu/ mongolia/section2a.shtml

2. Ray Huang, *China: A Macro History* (London: M.E. Sharpe, Inc., 1990), p. 138.

3. Robert Marshall, *Storm From the East: From Genghis Khan to Kublai Khan* (Berkeley: University of California, 1993), p. 48.

4. Jack Weatherford, *Genghis Khan and the Making of the Modern World* (New York: Random House, 2004), p. 160.

5. Ibid., 197.

6. Patricia Buckley Ebrey, *Cambridge Illustrated History of China* (London: Cambridge University Press, 1996), p.172.

7. Jehangir S. Pocha, "Mongolia Sees Genghis Khan's Good Side," *International Herald Tribune*, May 10, 2005, http://www.iht.com/articles/2005/05/09/news/mongol.php

8. Hideko Takayama, "The Bay Was Packed with Ships: How Did a Divine Wind Save Japan From Mongol Invaders 700 Years Ago?" *MSNBC Newsweek International Edition*, August 16, 2006, http://www.msnbc.msn.com/id/5635132/site/newsweek

9. Weatherford, p. 211.

10. Takayama.

Chapter 6. The Mughal Empire

1. John Keay, *India: A History* (New York: Atlantic Monthly Press, 2000), p. 292.

2. Stanley Wolpert, *A New History of India* (New York: Oxford University Press, 1977), p. 124.

3. Keay, p. 309.

4. Wolpert, p. 128.

5. Ibid., p. 132.

6. "The Mughals," Washington State University, World Civilizations, An Internet Classroom and Anthology, http://www.wsu.edu/~dee/MUGHAL/MUGHAL.HTM

7. John McLeod, *The History of India* (Westport, CT: Greenwood Press, 2002), p. 53.

8. Ibid., p. 55.

9. Akbar S. Ahmed, "The Taj Mahal," *History Today*, May 1993, p. 62.

10. Constantine Bond, "The Man Who Built the Taj," *Smithsonian*, August 1997, p. 56.

Chapter 7. Tibet (Tibet Autonomous Region—TAR)

1. Tsering Shakya, *The Dragon in the Land of Snows: A History of Modern Tibet Since 1947* (New York: Columbia University Press, 1999), p. 4.

2. Dalai Lama, *Freedom in Exile: The Autobiography of the Dalai Lama* (New York: Harper Collins, 1990), p. 12.

3. Ibid., p. 98.

4. Ibid., p. 132.

5. Hugh M. Richardson, *Tibet and Its History* (Boulder, CO: Shambala Publications, 1984), p. 211.

6. Eric S. Margolis, *War at the Top of the World: The Struggle for Afghanistan, Kashmir and Tibet* (New York: Routledge, 2000), p. 197.

7. Tim Johnson "China to Open Rail Link to Tibet, Easing Travel to Roof of the World," *Orlando Sentinel*, June 30, 2006, http://www.phayul.com/news/article.aspx?id=13075&t=1&c=1

8. The Government of Tibet in Exile, "Tibet at a Glance," http://www.tibet.com/glance.html

9. The Government of Tibet in Exile, "The Dalai Lama's Biography," http://www.tibet.com/DL/biography.html

10. The Government of Tibet in Exile, "Discovery of His Holiness the 14th Dalai Lama," http://www.tibet.com/DL/discovery.html

11. Dalai Lama, *Freedom In Exile: The Autobiography of the Dalai Lama* (New York: Harper Collins 1990), p. 12.

Chapter 8. The Empire of Japan

1. Naval Historical Center, "Pearl Harbor Raid, 7 December 1941," October 7, 2000, http://www.history.navy.mil/photos/events/wwii-pac/pearlhbr/pearlhbr.htm

2. James McClain, *A Modern History of Japan* (New York: W.W. Norton & Co., 2002), p. 482.

3. Ibid., p. 483.

4. Ibid., p. 334.

5. Ibid., p. 449.

6. "Unit 731: Japan's Biological Force," *BBC News World Edition*, February 1, 2002, http://news.bbc.co.uk/2/hi/programmes/correspondent/ 1796044.stm

7. McClain, p. 507.

8. Ibid., p. 513.

9. "The Atomic Bombings of Hiroshima and Nagasaki," The Avalon Project at Yale Law School, http://www.yale.edu/lawweb/avalon/abomb/mp10.htm

10. John Heresy, *Hiroshima* (New York: Vintage Books, 1989), p. 51.

11. U.S. Department of Energy, The Manhattan Project: An Interactive History, "The Atomic Bombing of Hiroshima," http://www.mbe.doe.gov/me70/manhattan/hiroshima.htm

Books

Black, Wallace B., and Jean F. Blashfield. *Hiroshima and the Atomic Bomb*. New York: Crestwood House, 1993.

Caputo, Philip. *Ten Thousand Days of Thunder: A History of the Vietnam War*. New York: Atheneum Books, 2005.

Duiker, William J. *Ho Chi Minh: A Life*. New York: Hyperion, 2000.

Greenblatt, Miriam. *Genghis Khan and the Mongol Empire*. Tarrytown, New York: Benchmark Books, 2002.

Heinrichs, Ann. *Tibet*. New York: Children's Press, 1996.

Lazo, Caroline. *The Terra Cotta Army of Emperor Qin*. New York: Discovery Books, 1993.

Moorecroft, Christine. *The Taj Mahal: How and Why It Was Built*. Austin, TX: Raintree Steck Vaughn Publishers, 1998.

Stein, R. Conrad. *World War II in the Pacific: Remember Pearl Harbor*. Hillside, New Jersey: Enslow Publishing, 1994.

Stewart, Whitney. *Aung San Suu Kyi: Fearless Voice of Burma*. Minneapolis: Lerner Publications Company, 1997.

Works Consulted

Aung San Suu Kyi. *Freedom From Fear and Other Writings*. London: Penguin, 1995.

Butler, David. *The Fall of Saigon*. New York: Simon & Schuster, 1985.

Chandler, David. *A History of Cambodia*. Sydney: Allen & Unwin, 1992.

———. *The Tragedy of Cambodian History: Politics, War and Revolution Since 1945*. New Haven, CT, Yale University Press, 1991.

Dalai Lama. *Freedom In Exile: The Autobiography of the Dalai Lama*. New York: Harper Collins 1990.

Ebrey, Patricia Buckley. *Cambridge Illustrated History of China*. London: Cambridge University Press, 1996.

Hauptly, Dennis J. *In Vietnam*. New York: Atheneum, 1985.

Heidhues, Mary Somers. *Southeast Asia: A Concise History*. London: Thames & Hudson, 2000.

Hersey, John. *Hiroshima*. New York: Vintage Books, 1989.

Huang, Ray. *China: A Macro History*. London: M.E. Sharpe, Inc., 1990.

Karnow, Stanley. *Vietnam: A History*. New York: Viking Press, 1983.

Keay, John. *India: A History*. New York: Atlantic Monthly Press, 2000.

Loung Ung. *First They Killed My Father: A Daughter of Cambodia Remembers*. New York: Harper Collins, 2000.

McClain, James. *A Modern History of Japan*. New York: W.W. Norton & Co., 2002.

Margolis, Eric S. *War at the Top of the World: The Struggle for Afghanistan, Kashmir and Tibet*. New York: Routledge, 2000.

Marshall, Robert. *Storm From the East: From Genghis Khan to Kublai Khan.* Berkeley: University of California, 1993.

Richardson, Hugh M. *Tibet and Its History.* Boulder, CO: Shambala Publications, 1984.

Tsering Shakya. *The Dragon in the Land of Snows: A History of Modern Tibet Since 1947.* New York: Columbia University Press, 1999.

Victor, Barbara. *The Lady: Aung San Suu Kyi Nobel Laureate and Burma's Prisoner.* Boston: Farber & Farber, 1998.

Weatherford, Jack. *Genghis Khan and the Making of the Modern World.* New York: Random House, 2004.

Wolpert, Stanley. *A New History of India.* New York: Oxford University Press, 1977.

Articles

Ahmed, Akbar S. "The Taj Mahal." *History Today,* May 1993.

The Avalon Project at Yale Law School: "The Atomic Bombings of Hiroshima and Nagasaki," http://www.yale.edu/lawweb/avalon/abomb/mp10.htm

BBC News: "Khmer Rouge 'Butcher' Ta Mok Dies," July 21, 2006, http://news.bbc.co.uk/2/hi/asia-pacific/5201770.stm

BBC News World Edition: "Unit 731: Japan's Biological Force," February 1, 2002, http://news.bbc.co.uk/2/hi/programmes/correspondent/1796044.stm

Bond, Constantine. "The Man Who Built the Taj." *Smithsonian,* August, 1997.

CNN.com: "Vietnam Marks Fall of Saigon," April 30, 2005, http://www.cnn.com/2005/WORLD/asiapcf/04/30/vietnam.anniversary

Emperor Qin's Terra-Cotta Warriors and Horses Museum, http://211.147.225.34/gate/big5/www.bmy.com.cn/english/bwgjs/l2p.htm

Esper, George. ABC News: "Fall of Saigon Remembered Anew," April 28, 2005, http://abcnews.go.com/International/print?id=710508

The Government of Tibet in Exile, http://www.tibet.com/index.html

Johnson, Tim. "China to Open Rail Link to Tibet, Easing Travel to Roof of the World." *Orlando Sentinel,* June 30, 2006.

Karnow, Stanley. TIME 100: Ho Chi Minh, "He married nationalism to communism and perfected the deadly art of guerilla warfare," http://www.time.com/time/time100/leaders/profile/hochiminh.html

Kirsten Scharnberg, "Last One to Leave and Frantic Last Mission With Ambassador," Fall of Saigon Marine Association, April 30, 2005, http://www.fallofsaigon.org/lastoleave_frantic_mission.htm

Loven, Jennifer. "Bush Compares U.S. Wars in Vietnam, Iraq," *U.S. News and World Report,* Nov. 17, 2006, http://www.redorbit.com/news/general/734999/bush_compares_us_wars_in_vietnam_iraq/index.html

Mazzatenta, O. Louis. "China's Warriors Rise From the Earth." *National Geographic,* October, 1996.

Ministry of Tourism: Cambodia Home of World Heritage. "A Brief History of Our Kingdom," http://www.mot.gov.kh/history.asp

Minnesota State University, Mankato: Emuseum, "Qin Dynsasty," http://www.mnsu.edu/emuseum/prehistory/china/early_imperial_china/qin.html

"The Mughals." Washington State University: World Civilizations. http://www.wsu.edu/~dee/MUGHAL/MUGHAL.HTM

Naval Historical Center, "Pearl Harbor Raid, 7 December 1941," October 7, 2000, http://www.history.navy.mil/photos/events/wwii-pac/pearlhbr/pearlhbr.htm

New York Times Travel Guides: Hanoi, "Ho Chi Minh's Mausoleum," http://travel.nytimes.com/travel/guides/asia/vietnam/hanoi/attraction-detail.html?vid=1154654613651&inline=nyt-classifier

Pocha, Jehangir S. "Mongolia Sees Genghis Khan's Good Side," *International Herald Tribune*, May 10, 2005, http://www.iht.com/articles/2005/05/09/news/mongol.php

Suu Kyi's Detention Extended, Supporters Likely to Protest," *The Irrawaddy News Magazine* Online Edition, May 27, 2006, http://www.Irrawaddy.org/aviewer.asp?a=5797&z=154

Takayama, Hideko. "The Bay Was Packed with Ships: How Did a Divine Wind Save Japan From Mongol Invaders 700 Years Ago?" *MSNBC Newsweek International Edition*, August 16, 2006, http://www.msnbc.msn.com/id/5635132/site/newsweek

U.S. Department of Energy: The Manhattan Project, An Interactive History, "The Atomic Bombing of Hiroshima," http://www.mbe.doe.gov/me70/manhattan/hiroshima.htm

University of Pennsylvania Museum of Archaeology and Anthropology, "Modern Mongolia: Reclaiming Genghis Khan," http://www.museum.upenn.edu/mongolia/section2a.shtml

University of Texas at Austin: "The Mausoleum of Qin Shi Huangdi," http://www.utexas.edu/courses/wilson/ant304/biography/arybios98/smithbio.html

On the Internet

Ancient Worlds: The Orient, http://www.ancientworlds.net/aw/city/286736

Burma Watch International, http://www.burmawatch.org/index.html

Explore the Taj Mahal, http://www.taj-mahal.net/augEng/main_screen.htm

Hiroshima Peace Site: The Official Homepage of the Hiroshima Peace Memorial Museum, http://www.pcf.city.hiroshima.jp/top_e.html

PBS: Vietnam Passage, "Journeys from War to Peace," http://www.pbs.org/vietnampassage/index.html

Royal Alberta Museum: Virtual Exhibits. Genghis Khan, http://www.royalalbertamuseum.ca/vexhibit/genghis/intro.htm

alliances (uh-LIE-un-suhs)—Close agreements among people, groups and nations for a common purpose.

autonomous (ah-TAH-nuh-mus)—Having the right to self-govern.

cavalry (KAA-vul-ree)—Soldiers on horseback.

civil war—War between opposing groups of people in the same country.

communist (KAH-myoo-nist)—A type of government that abolishes private property, such as the former Soviet Union and the present-day People's Republic of China.

Dalai Lama (DAH-lay LAH-mah)—The spiritual leader of Tibetan Buddhism.

democracy (duh-MAA-kruh-see)—A system of government in which the people elect their leaders and vote on the laws of the land.

dynasty (DYE-nuh-stee)—Rule that is passed through the same family, from one generation to the next.

economic depression (eh-kuh-NAH-mik dee-PREH-SHUN)—A severe decrease in business activity, with a lasting drop in incomes.

empire—A collection of territories, kingdoms, or nations controlled by one central authority.

evacuation (ee-VAA-kyoo-AY-shun—The removal of people from a particular place, usually for their safety.

fascist (FAA-shist)—A dictator-type government, such as Germany and Italy before and during World War II.

guerrilla (guh-RIL-uh) **warfare**—Fighting done by small groups of people using hit-and-run tactics to defeat a much larger enemy force.

kamikaze (kah-muh-KAH-zee)—A Japanese word that means "Divine Wind," it is a suicidal attack on the enemy, or a soldier who performs such a suicidal attack. It also applies to a typhoon.

mausoleum (maw-suh-LEE-um)—A large tomb, usually above ground.

mortar—A type of cannon with a short barrel that fires shells at very steep angles. Also, the shells fired from such a cannon.

Nazi (NOT-zee)—The fascist government of Germany just before and during World War II.

nomadic (noh-MAA-dik)—Moving from place to place in order to live off the land.

pro—In support of something or someone.

province (PRAH-vins)—A specific section of a country or empire, similar to a state in the United States.

subcontinent (sub-KAN-tih-nent)—A large landmass that is part of a continent.

typhoon (tye-FOON)—A hurricane in the western Pacific Ocean.

About the Author

Photo by Greg Dillon

Doug Dillon lives in the Orlando, Florida, area, where he writes for both young people and adults. His background includes nearly twenty years' experience teaching geography and history, as well as working directly with high-risk youth, in grades 7 to 12. In a cooperative effort with a seventh-grade-level team of teachers, he and his associates received the prestigious Disney Teacherrific Award. In a series of five articles for *Boys' Life* magazine, SIRS (Social Issues Resource Series) selected two of Doug's articles, "Gentle Pioneer" and "Boys of the Civil War," as reference works. Harcourt Assessment, Inc., also chose one of those articles, "Walt Disney: America's Fun Maker," for use in the Michigan Educational Assessment Program from 2007 to 2015. Doug Dillon is a member of the Society of Children's Book Writers and Illustrators.